TIME TO START

Your Art

Learn to Paint with Passion

SUE TRUSLER

Welcome to the world of Art. I started painting when I retired. Sharing illustrations of my art journey, I would like to show you how to enjoy your art. For those with little or no knowledge of painting, it's amazing what can be achieved, just by having the courage to make a start. I have developed a passion for art which I am keen to share. Paint to please yourself and your passion and skills will grow. It's not about perfection, your creativity is the key to enjoying your art.

Sue Trusler

Chapter 1 Canal Art
Painting Canal Art Roses on a narrowboat in acrylics.

Chapter 2 Botanical Beauty
Introduction to Botanical Art with watercolours.

Chapter 3 Sketching Skills
How sketching jam jars can lead to drawing mansions.

Chapter 4 Watercolour Weekend
Paint anything in watercolour from feathers to lakes.

Chapter 5 Loose Florals
Large creative flowers with masking fluid and inks.

Chapter 6 What's Out There
Where to find classes, courses, free tuition and more.

Chapter 7 Exhibition Excitement
Learn about how to display your art.

Chapter 8 Talking Art
Art materials explained, with different paints and brushes required by chapter from 1to5.

Chapter 1
Canal Art

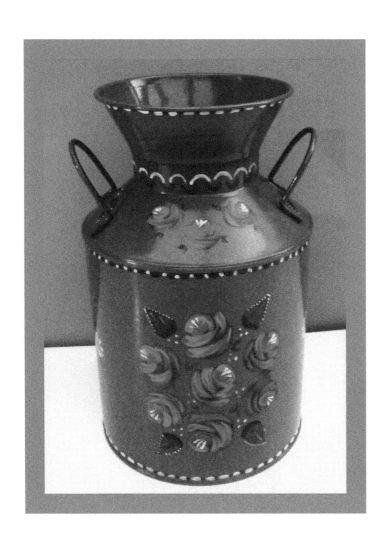

If I can paint, so can you. Art has become my greatest passion, by sharing my artistic journey, let me ignite your desire to paint. A very unexpected chain of events, took me from wobbly brush strokes, to confidently exhibiting and writing about my art. After 37 years in Finance, I retired and suddenly woke up to the joy of painting.

Purchasing a small narrow boat with my husband Bob, there was an expectation of relaxing cruises and time to appreciate a slower pace of life, but fate played a wild card. Our pre loved boat was in a good state of repair, just the perfect size for two people, but it was covered in dolphins. They were leaping around the engine box, diving past palm trees on the side of the cabin, covering the tiles around the galley and frosted onto the bathroom window. We decided if we hadn't spotted any dolphins after navigating the length of the Monmouthshire & Brecon canal then the dolphins would have to go! This little boat was crying out for a makeover, to restore her traditional narrowboat character. With no prior knowledge of boat restoration, it was quite easy to research the right type of paint and how to apply it. The hull needed stripping back and then any minor areas of rust were treated prior to the application of a beautiful, creamy textured undercoat of battleship grey. The texture was so smooth it went on like a dream. Three shades of specialist high gloss boat paint were selected, Squall, Mauritius and Sapphire. The only problem was finding someone to paint the Canal Art roses. There were assorted vinyl stickers online, but they looked mass produced and lacked character. Unable to find a Canal Artist locally, after a great deal of research, a book was found on how to paint traditional roses and castles. With nothing to lose, I decided to give it a try. So began my art journey.

As we wanted roses on both the inside and outside of the doors, watercolour paint wasn't an option. After some deliberation I settled for acrylic paint. The beauty of this was it dried relatively quickly and light colours could be applied over dark. No amount of reading was going to suddenly enable me to paint roses. Having purchased a set of basic acrylic colours and a set of suitable brushes, I began to "learn by doing".

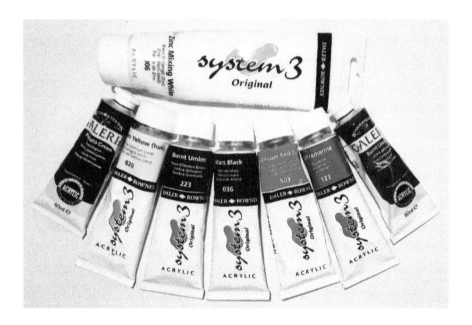

The start point for each rose was a basic circle, somewhat easier said than done. My hands were very adept at creating egg shapes and ovals but not circles. Years of problem solving during my working life, had fortunately left its mark.

There had to be a reason I wasn't making circles. Being right-handed, if I painted in a clockwise direction, I ended up masking my shape. Painting a circle anti clockwise I could see the shape emerging. Probably not a recognised artists way of doing things, but it worked for me. Following some basic guidance for regularly rinsing my brush in water, to stop it clogging, was helpful. However, nothing beats trying to do something yourself and then figuring out what's best for you.

Having mastered the initial circle, once that was dried, I needed a smaller slightly darker circle, placed near the perimeter of my first circle. Confident with painting circles, this was quite an easy step to take.

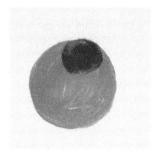

Patiently waiting for everything to dry, gave time to clean brushes and choose my colours for the petals. Many years ago, when families lived and worked on long barges, the women were very proud of the traditional art, which gave their working home an identity. Different artists would have their own individual style, a particular number of petals, certain patterns on leaves and different picture designs. Collectively all looked similar, they were individually quite unique.

With this in mind, I needed to find my own "rose". One that could be reproduced over and over again, with a variety of colours and different sizes, facing up, down or sideways. First attempts at petals, gripping the brush tightly near the bottom and slowly wobbling along, didn't really look very attractive. Further attempts became even more stilted and harsh. Time to tap into my old analytical mind. Looking at examples, the petals were made with sweeping and fluid lines. I needed to find the confidence to loosen up and speed up. Just like putting a tick in an exercise book. If you try drawing a slow tick it looks so odd, but rush in with a quick flick of the pen and you create a confident sweeping tick. Apply this to painting rose petals and you're onto a winner.

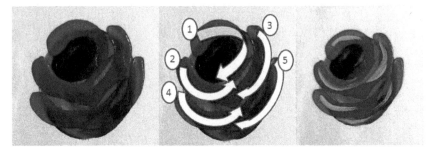

With the petals in place and enhanced with highlights, all that remains to be done is the stamens.

It took a while to figure out how to paint roses and some of my initial attempts were very faltering. The top three examples, were when my hand was gripping the brush tightly and I was attempting to create shapes with wobbly movements.

I also experimented with the number and shape of my petals. Progressing to the three lower roses, I had come closer to my own petal shape and started to loosen my grip and speed up my brush strokes.

Learning by doing is a really powerful process. The above roses show an emerging style and improvement. Looking back, I am so glad that I had the confidence to experiment and have a go.

Don't be tempted to give up after your first attempt.

If I can paint, so can you. Just practice at your own pace, enjoy the moment and you will improve. I am so glad that I took pictures along the way as it would be impossible to replicate my first roses.

With our little boat stripped back, the last of the dolphins on the paintwork were erased, just leaving inside the bathroom window.

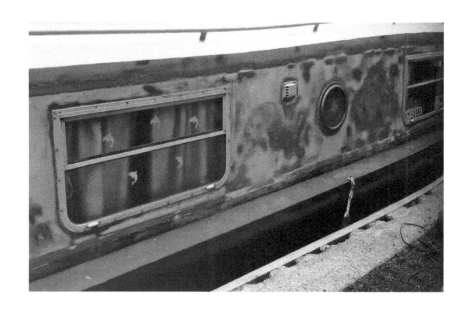

Painting the undercoat of creamy battleship grey, started her transformation.

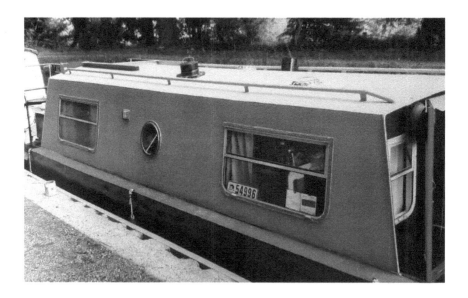

The new blues were applied in stages. It was not the easiest thing to do, as the boat had to remain in the water. Fine weather was needed but not too warm, or the paint would dry out. It's amazing how hot a steel boat becomes in the sunshine.

Several weeks of driving back and forth to the canal and we were ready to remove the front and back doors for the final step of our restoration. Plywood doors were installed as a temporary measure. By now I had painted so many roses, my concern was about what design to paint, not could I paint the roses. As well as roses, the same process of "learn by doing" had been followed for leaves and daisies, two other key elements of Canal Art.

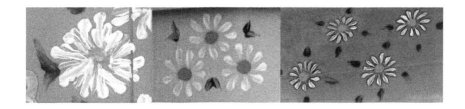

Turning our conservatory into a workshop, the doors were sanded down and painted in Sapphire blue. With the paint thoroughly dried, tiny sticky dots were applied to position the centre of each rose. Painting the initial circles, the dots were removed. With the design mapped out using the roses, the leaves and daisies were painted on by eye. This helped retain the fluid, hand painted style.

The process had to be repeated to produce the same pattern on the inside, which would be on show when the doors were open.

Once completed the acrylic paint was allowed to thoroughly dry and a coat of varnish applied over the whole door surface. It was such an exciting and satisfying day when the doors were finally put back on our boat. As we cruised on the canal, we had many admiring glances, with people commenting on how pretty our boat was. Having "Rosie & Jim" on the front seats, brought a lot of smiles. We had many conversations with strangers, about their childhood memories of the children's TV series about Rosie & Jim's adventures on the narrowboat "Ragdoll".

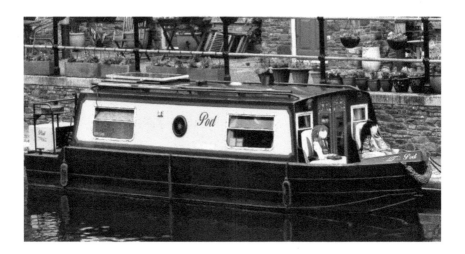

We met an American family with a hire boat, about three times the length of our little Pod. Being moored up near each other, they asked if they could take some pictures of our quaint boat.

Chatting about my artwork, we ended up eating together at an old canal side pub. The following day we helped them to negotiate their first lock. Quite an experience with an extremely long hire boat.

Many photos of our boat, have been included with happy holiday memories of people from near and far. Our biggest "paparazzi" moment was when we were moored at a beautiful spot by Brynich Aqueduct. Being in the middle of the countryside, we were reliant on a standby canned curry for lunch. Just as we were about to sit out with our picnic table, the Dragonfly Cruise boat moored up and a party of tourists disembarked.

The plates of curry were hastily put back inside as we moved out of the way, allowing the happy tourists to enjoy photographing our boat. It was customary for the trip boat to pass through the lock, over the aqueduct and allow passengers to disembark whilst the boat used the turning point, ready to head back to Brecon. Usually, visitors took pictures from the viaduct, of the river below and the beautiful rolling countryside. On this occasion, their first photo shoot was our boat. Thankfully, Rosie & Jim were on board, whilst we kept well out of sight. The curry had to be warmed back up, but we were thankful we had managed to evade the cameras, whilst providing the tourists with some interesting memories of their canal trip in Wales.

Continuing my new found passion, after the initial challenge learning to paint canal roses on our boat, further opportunities to paint beckoned. Now totally hooked on painting roses, the next step was to experiment with different shapes and surfaces. The doors were relatively simple, being flat and made of wood. Milk churns and watering cans were a whole different story.

Painting on a curved metal surface, took me back to rather hesitant brushstrokes. More pressure was needed to keep the brush in contact with the curved surface. Too much pressure would make the paint flow in stripes.

Luckily, it's easy to wipe paint off with an old cloth and start again. The tiny sticky dots were invaluable for marking out a design, as it's impossible to see right around a curved object. Yet it was easy enough to measure the circumference with a tailor's tape measure, then space out dots for the rose centres.

Lots of different shaped objects provided endless opportunities to create new designs. Unlike matching the doors, with no need to keep patterns similar, it was great fun to look at an item and try out slight variations of colour and size of roses. Embracing the creativity of painting, means you have the freedom to do whatever pleases you. There is no truer meaning to being creative, than putting your own stamp on something.

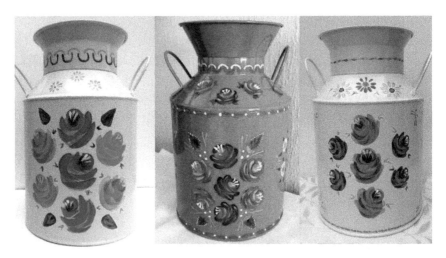

Fate having dealt the need for roses to be painted on a boat, next led me to a magazine about Painting and Drawing. With lots of guidance and information, it also featured readers art. After reading several issues, I hadn't seen anything that remotely resembled a Canal Art rose.

With nothing to lose, I decided to submit some photos of my work and a brief outline on how I started painting my boat.

Much to my surprise, I received an email asking for some further photos, as my art was going to be featured on two pages.

Feeling confident about painting, having developed your style, the next step is to feel confident about others looking at your work. It's amazing how many people will be drawn to your art, and really love it. At the very worst they may not like it, but that is no reflection on your skill, just personal preference. Some people like opera and others heavy rock, but neither is right or wrong. Whether you paint Canal Art, portraits, landscapes, abstract shapes, your art will be appreciated by some and dismissed by others. It took me a while to understand this. Once I realised anyone who expresses their creativity through painting is called an artist, my confidence grew.

Paint to please yourself and your passion and skills will grow.

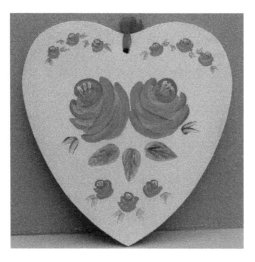

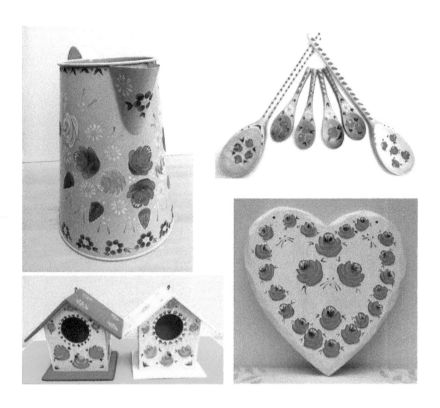

With all manner of objects lovingly adorned in roses, there became a bit of a storage issue. If an art magazine thought my work was good enough to put onto two pages, then maybe people would like to own some of it.

A friend mentioned that there was to be an event at the Canal Lock Centre. Enquiries made, resulting in a space being purchased to sell my work. It was rather stressful, packing everything to avoid any damage on the car journey, making sure we had sufficient coins and wondering if anyone would want to purchase anything. With a few minor panics, the event went quite smoothly and people bought hearts to hang on their walls, pots to hold indoor plants as well as little mementos of their canal side outing. It was nice to meet people and led to participating in other craft fairs.

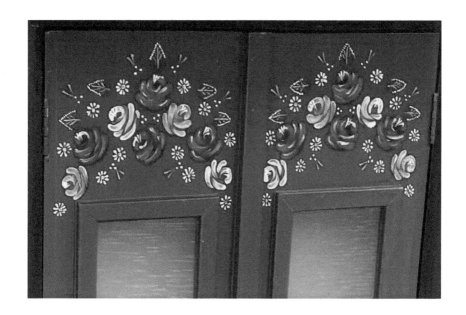

From this opening chapter, it's easy to see if you can take the first step to starting your art, all manner of other things can magically happen. My first step was with Canal Art, but you can start anywhere. Watercolour flowers, acrylic landscapes, pet portraits, farm animals, still life, beautiful buildings, the list is as long as you care to make it.

Read on, to find out how I took up watercolour painting and the great opportunities that opened up, to be creative and enjoy my art. Needless to say there some interesting events and wobbly moments. All part of the fun.

Chapter 2
Botanical Beauty

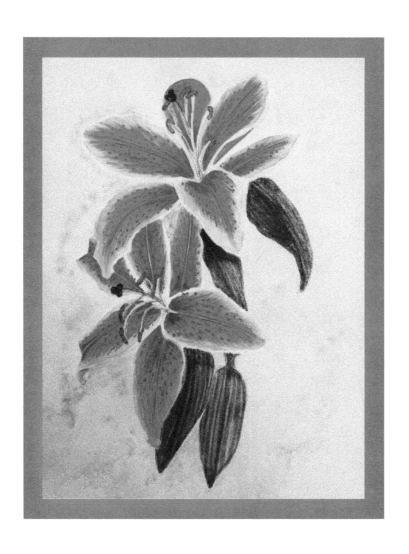

One of the best things about retirement is the time available to pursue wish list activities. The dreams that used to be put to one side, on hold, when life was running away, with all sorts of things that needed attention. Days from the wish list were now possible, which was how I came to be strolling around Dyffryn Gardens. As a National Trust site, it had a large arboretum, greenhouse, kitchen garden, a delightful assortment of themed walled gardens and an old mansion. The house was gradually being restored and there were often exhibitions on the ground floor. It had been the home of the well known coal and shipping magnate John Cory and was the height of fashion in the Edwardian Era.

A love of flowers led to entering the downstairs dining room, where there was a display of botanical art. Spellbound by the beauty and detail of the pieces, I slowly advanced around the room. A lot of the flowers that could be seen growing in the gardens, had been magically captured on paper and hung for all to admire. Knowing how long it had taken to produce canal roses, I was in awe of the delicate brushstrokes, subtlety of colour and attention to the minutest of detail in these paintings. Eventually reaching the end of the exhibition, there was a notice offering a one day introduction to botanical art. Fate was playing a wild card yet again. Although not even a beginner, I decided that there would be nothing to lose by attending. After all, I had been fascinated by the paintings and at the very least would like to know how they had been created.

Details noted down, a place was secured the following day for a one day course in two weeks' time. This gave ample opportunity to look up the Artist.

Viewing some more of her work gave me an insight into her botanical art style.

On the day, it was only a short drive to Insole Court Mansion. Another old property, which had been rescued and restored, with a vast amount of fundraising via the local community. James Harvey Insole, started to build a family home in Llandaff, Cardiff in the mid-1800s. As with many such properties, after the first World War, fortunes declined and the mansion and grounds were eventually taken over by the local council. In 1988 a local action group was set up to save the property and land from being sold to developers. After many years of campaigning, Insole Court is now at the heart of the community, with all buildings restored. The kitchen gardens are now maintained as allotments, the surrounding grounds are maintained with the help of volunteers. Stables and outhouses have been sympathetically restored externally, whilst becoming studios and class rooms. All sorts of activities take place at this hub, including the Botanical Art for Beginners class.

Having located the stable room, upon entering, I found two ladies busying themselves with jam jars containing lots of different flowers, as well as some rather dead looking specimens. Asking if I was too early, one of the ladies said to take a seat, as everything was almost ready. She introduced herself as Debbie, our tutor. There had been a slight delay on the motorway, so she was just on the final touches, setting up the room. The other lady was a regular pupil, who liked the buzz of tutorial days. Soon several others came to occupy the seats and informal introductions took place. This was so nice, as I was concerned that Botanical Art being so precise, may have had a very prim and proper tutor, with a strict etiquette for questions or interacting.

Probably, I was thinking back several decades ago, to Latin lessons at school.

Debbie was so friendly and sociable, admitting a total addiction to coffee before she could really settle into the day. Without any more ado, orders were taken around the table and passed onto the café staff. What a great way to feel at ease with strangers and nip any apprehension in the bud. With cappuccinos, lattes and americanos all claimed, it was time to start learning about Botanical Art.

Debbie began painting flowers at the very early age of six, copying watercolour illustrations of her grandmothers. Once her passion was ignited, she continued to attain a Diploma in Botanical Illustration from the English Gardening School at the Chelsea Physic Garden. This was no mean feat. Listening to her background was a great way to be introduced to Botanical Art, in a small, cosy environment, with someone very willing to share her years of experience.

A little of the history, told us that botanical art had started way back in ancient Greece, using illustrations to identify plants. Hence the very great attention to detail. Prior to the invention of the camera, using illustrations was the only way to identify thousands of individual plant species. Verbal or written descriptions were open to various interpretation, but botanical illustrations represented exactly what the eye saw.

This was the key to our day, observation.

Our first exercise was to look at fir tree cones, to observe the Fibonacci sequence in Nature. There are endless books and theories written about Fibonacci numbers, but thankfully our only need was to observe the patterns, following the sequence.

As well as the spiral pattern on the cones, the vast majority of flowers have a number of petals that follow the sequence of 1,3,5,8,13 etc. Calla Lilies have 1 leaf, Iris 3, Buttercups 5, Delphiniums 8 and Corn Marigold 13.

Debbie demonstrated how to draw the spiral patterns in pencil. When satisfied with the drawing, it could be traced over with a fine permanent black ink pen. Allowing for the ink to fully dry, erasing the pencil, layers of watercolour could be applied. Following Debbie's guidance, it was surprising how well our first attempts turned out.

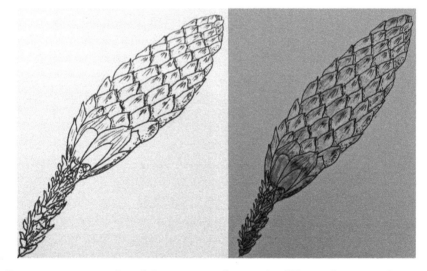

Once your eye is able to see the spiralling shapes, it becomes much easier to draw. The big question to ask; could someone find this species of Proteus fir cone, just by using my botanical art.

Keen observation had enabled everyone to make a very reasonable illustration. We all became fascinated at observing things, marvelling at Fibonacci's findings.

Out of interest, you can observe the number of petals on the following plants.

Then look to see how they overlap or stay separate from each other. The third thing to look at is the centre of the bloom. No need to drag your mind back to biology lessons, to recall which part is the stamen, stigma, anther or sepal. Although nice to know, the names are not required, what is needed is the ability to look at how many parts there are. How tall or short the parts are, do they bend or are they straight.

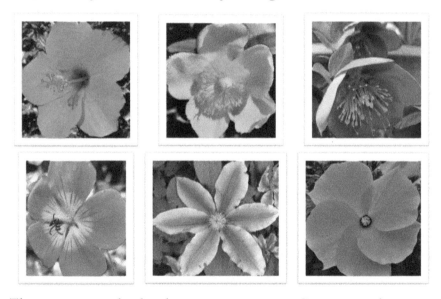

The more you look, the more you see. Some petals are wide open whilst others are curled inwards. The centre of these flowers, although serving the same purpose, are all very different in size and form. Once you start to identify these differences, each flower becomes unique, so drawing it becomes less of a task.

Before you lift a pencil, check out the number of petals, how they touch or separate from each other.
Identify the overall shape, so an outline can be softly drawn as a guide.

Since starting to learn Botanical Art, I have taken thousands of photographs whilst visiting National Trust Gardens and Heritage sites. The more pictures you take from different angles, the better understanding you develop, for the structure of individual blooms.

It's also interesting to take apart a flower and lay it out on a white sheet of paper. After a while you get used to looking at lots of flowers, so it becomes second nature to observe all the key elements. These examples are slightly more complex. Where there are lots of petals, not all will be in view, so it is just the feeling of multiple petals that needs to be captured, there is no need to capture every single one.

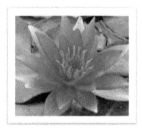 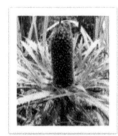 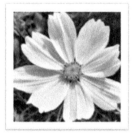

Although the number of pink leaves could possibly be counted, only you would know the exact figure, for those that could be seen. The lilac example is quite fluffy in appearance, this is what needs to be portrayed rather than detailing every individual part. The most significant part is the centre, which would need more accuracy. The white petals can easily be counted, so any painting should show all eight petals. Keen obsevation will show how the petals are placed, do they all overlap one another or are some closer to the centre. resting on others.

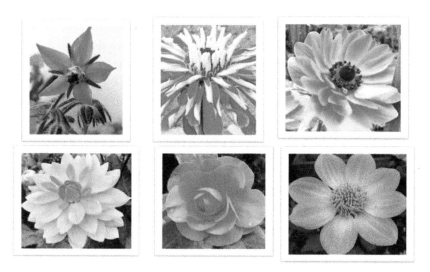

It's easy to see the vast differences in the above flowers.

In the painting below the flowers all have the same number of petals, clearly belonging to the same plant, but each is a slightly different colour or shape.

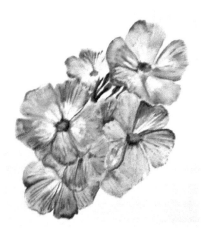

The next challenge to our observational skills was to select some of Debbie's "dried" examples. Some were quite alien in appearance, but proved to be excellent for learning to draw.

As they were not familiar, such as bluebells or poppies, we had to look at them, rather than just glance, filling in the rest with preconceived memories.

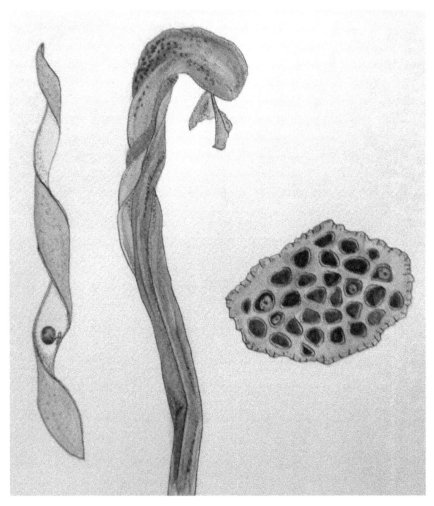

Although not the pretty botanical flowers we had expected to be painting, it was a very good exercise in observation and attention to detail.

By no means perfect, our botanical illustrations were sufficient to identify the specimens we had endevoured to capture. The silver spiral Wisteria Pod, green & brown mottled Sarracenia and the Lotus Seed Head.

The morning had somehow flown by and it was time for lunch. With so much learnt, there was a lot to chat about, as the group made their way to the small restaurant. Forgoing deserts, take away coffees were purchased with everyone eager to return to the classroom. Debbie explained a few techniques and showed some of her beautiful botanical art. We were then asked to select a flower for our afternoon session. With foxgloves being one of my favourite flowers, I picked a stem and placed it in front of me.

With Debbies guidance, stems and blooms were rotated to be observed from a pleasing angle, then taped to stay in position. The process of observation, outlining the shape then filling the detail, produced a pencil drawing that could then be made permanent with indian ink markers. This was the beginners process for producing botanical art. Debbie advised that with growing confidence, a far more detailed painting could be achieved without the use of ink.

As with everything, master the basics and you have a great foundation to move forward from. At the end of one day, everyone was really pleased with their art work and keen to start putting their skills into practice.

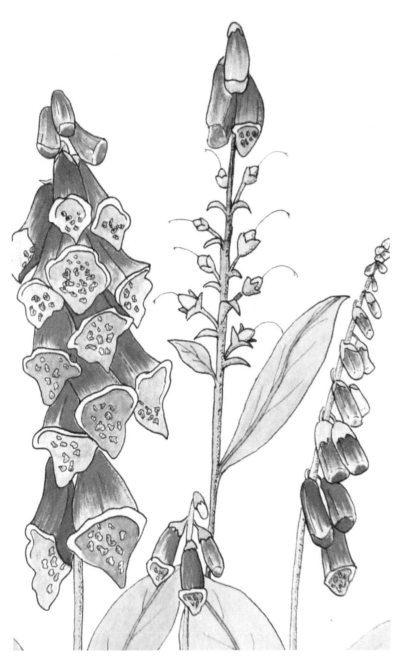

First Foxgloves

I was hooked on watercolour. Adding water made the colour turn lighter, some colours were opaque, others transparent or semi-transparent. They could be mixed together, to create all sorts of colours and shades. The names were so pretty, quinacridone gold, rose madder, phthalo blue, imperial purple.

At this point, with a great desire to paint flowers in watercolour, I was suddenly overwhelmed. How to learn all the names let alone their properties, which ones to mix together, to create the right colours for leaves or petals. What size brushes to use, sable or synthetic, round or pointed? What type of paper, Hot Pressed (HP), Not Hot Pressed (NOT), my lack of knowledge was breath-taking. With my analytical skills taking over, I pored over lists of names, only to find there were different makes of paint, Windsor Newton, Daniel Smith, Sennelier, Shinhan. Even worse, the same colours in different makes were not all equal, some could granulate, others were creamier or didn't mix so well.

Fortunately, after hours grappling with all of these issues, I decided to just sit down and follow the process that Debbie had outlined. She had suggested a few main colours and had said a lot was down to personal preference. The greatest piece of advice I so wish I'd been given is "Learn by Doing". As children we learnt to sing "Happy Birthday" before we could read the words, understood the alphabet, or had any knowledge of musical notation, treble or bass clef. Yet we learnt to sing. To enjoy painting for pleasure, you don't need to know all the technical bits. As you progress, you may choose to learn certain things, to study a particular aspect of painting, but choose do this when you are ready. Don't put unnecessary pressure on yourself.

Professionals can spend years at University studying art, but to start enjoying painting, all you need are a few paints, some brushes and watercolour paper.

Having got over my "analytical phase", I decided to attend another Beginners Botanical Art Day with Debbie. This time I took some notes, really paid attention to observing the flowers and dried seed pods, so thoroughly enjoyed the day. The class was small, allowing time for personal guidance. Whilst processes were reaffirmed, with different flowers and informal tuition, it didn't feel like a repeat of my first session. There was so much to learn and enjoy.

I went on to attend a few more sessions with Debbie, as there was always something different to focus on. Her teaching embedded the basics, whilst providing tailored guidance, to assist individual progress. Her informal, relaxed manner enabled her pupils to feel at ease and therefore gain confidence in their painting

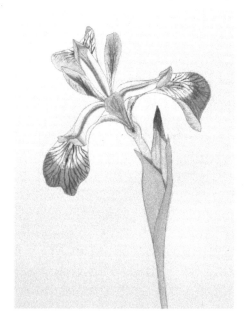

That summer, Bob and I finally made it to the Chelsea Flower Show. It was a fabulous day, so sunny and bright. My love of painting had really opened my eyes, to appreciate the delicate detail of all the different varieties of flowers. Whilst totally absorbed in a display of Orchids, I was approached by a representative of the Orchid Society of Great Britain. In conversation with experts, I have found it best to admit a total lack of knowledge rather than be caught out. I explained that my interest in Orchids stemmed from recently taking up Botanical Art.

The lady advised me that for a small membership fee, the OSGB had a quarterly journal, with lots of beautiful pictures of Orchids from around the world. As well as holding meetings and having competitions for growing Orchids, they also held an annual photography and art competition. This was an opportunity not to be missed, loving a challenge; my membership form was swiftly completed. Probably the last thing I would have imagined joining, at the start of the day. My success at growing flowers, being equal to my ability to win a marathon. However, if I put my mind to it, I could certainly enter the OSGB art competition.

There was one particular Orchid that caught my eye, as it had a very unusual structure. Deciding to take several extra photographs, an idea was forming somewhere that this could be a good specimen to paint. With a few months to practice, as the entry date drew near, I was quite pleased with my submission.

The judging was to take place at the December meeting in London, so I arranged to post my painting to the organiser. Having taken so long over its creation, the packaging was proportionately time consuming.

Years of posting surprise packages to our daughter in university paid dividends. Layers of card and bubble wrap, secured with yards of parcel tape, ensuring the safe arrival of my Orchid artwork.

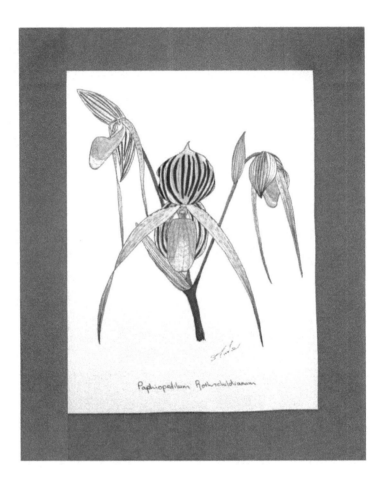

Paphiopedilum Rothschildianum

Having produced a painting that I felt was worthy of submission, it was quite exciting and rewarding.

To find I had been placed 3rd in the amateur art competition was almost unbelievable, particularly as my orchid wasn't the prettiest of specimens, having been chosen for its relatively easy structure.

The following year I entered 3 paintings and was awarded 2nd and 3rd place. In conversation with one of the committees, I agreed to write an article for the OSGB Journal, encouraging people to try painting and to enter the art competition. There were lots of photographic entries but fewer in the art section.

I took the line that the click of a shutter, only takes a split second. To draw or paint an orchid, takes time to look at the structure, observe the flower, to fully appreciate the delicate detail and subtleties of the plant. I had become very passionate about painting Orchids; the more I looked at them, the more I appreciated the uniqueness of each variety. Choosing a very simple example, I gave a brief guide on how to observe and draw the basic structure, outline with a fine permanent ink line, then add watercolours.

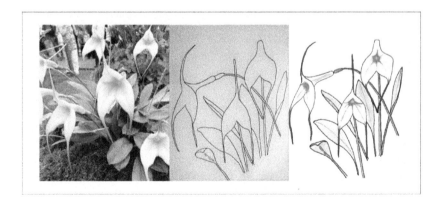

After first been shown an OSGB Journal at Chelsea, I had now contributed an article encouraging people to try painting orchids.

This did bring to mind the saying "shooting yourself in the foot".

I was encouraging entries, when I was pushing myself to improve my own art work, trying to achieve 1st place.

Putting quality over quantity, I focused on creating one entry. Experience had taught me, that poetic licence was a key element of art. Often striving to produce a near photographic replica of a flower, when the only person to see the original flower would be me. No one would know where every petal fell or each leaf was positioned.

Purchasing a beautiful pink orchid, I studied it from all angles. Sketching out some different designs, deciding upon one that showed front, side and back views of the flowers. Each individual bloom was correctly represented, but brought together to create a pleasing painting.

Learn by doing, being my mantra, I looked at my previous year's entry and could see how much my work had improved. All by gaining confidence, painting regularly, getting to know how my paints flowed on different paper and most importantly, enjoying becoming comfortable with my own creativity.

Having taken two and a half years, to secure 1st place, my sense of achievement was such a lovely reward.

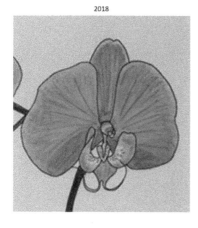
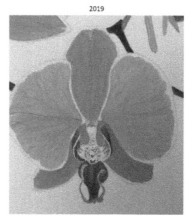

Even if you never choose to enter a competition, if you take pictures of your art, it becomes very rewarding to see your improvement. Hesitant to say practice makes perfect, I can confirm without shadow of a doubt, that practice shows improvement and creates a great sense of achievement. Just a couple of hours a week painting, can provide relaxation and enjoyment, releasing your creativity. Without even realising it, your painting will improve.

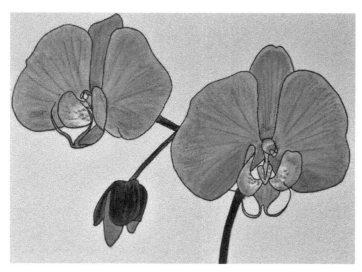

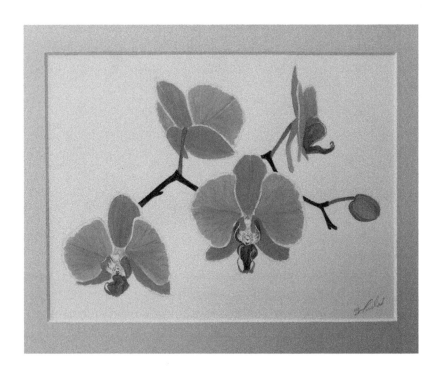

My winning entry had some easily noticeable improvements, can you spot them?

There was no longer a black outline to the flowers and stems. The composition showed front, side and back views, whilst looking quite natural. Greater observation on the thickness and colour of the stems, turning from brown to a lighter shade when connecting with the flower. Improved blending of colour in petals to give a far more delicate appearance.

All these enhancements took time, I am still working to improve my art. Approaching art with a positive attitude is a great help. Don't look for mistakes, just see opportunities to do things a little differently next time. Why stand still when you can enjoy seeing continuous progress.

Chapter 3
Sketching Skills

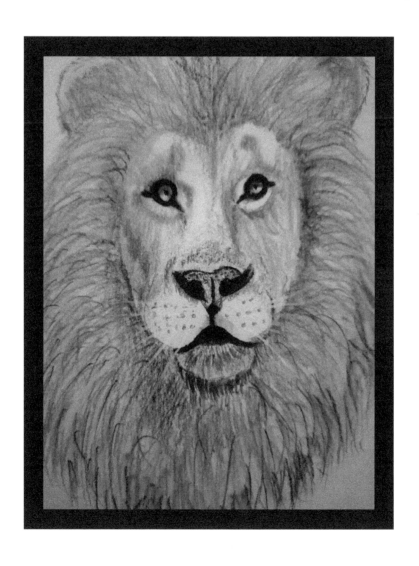

Sometimes a small chain of events leads to something very special. Retirement provided the opportunity to meet with an old school friend. A single meeting became a regular event that led to the discovery of an exercise class, at a local community hub. The class was at 10am which gave ample opportunity afterwards to relax over coffee. Buzzing with chatter, the Hub Cafe was located in the main hall of a very solid grey stone building, a Grammar School from a previous decade. As The Hub, it now hosted a number of exercise classes, music lessons, drama workshops and community singing groups.

In the main, people turned up for the exercise class alone or with a friend, stood in their usual spot and departed when the class finished. On the occasion that the instructor's car broke down, conversation began between the class members, whilst waiting in the corridor. Through common ground, initial speculation on where out teacher was, broke the ice. Leading on to other areas of common interest, resulted in an invitation to join up for coffee, being extended to the group. Over the next few weeks, one by one ladies stayed on for a coffee and got to know one another. Friendly conversation spanned a wide range of interesting and diverse topics.

During one coffee conversation, reference was made to a rescued Victorian Mansion, on the other side of the city, where a day time Pilate's class had started. Two ladies had just joined, who were also interested in the evening classes, one of which was a ten-week introduction to drawing. As the winter evenings brought darkness, shortening the days, it sounded like a promising alternative to staying at home, sunk into an armchair watching TV.

Had I been sitting at the other end of the group; this piece of light conversation may have passed me by. Fortunately, being in the right place, enabled a mental note to be made, to explore this opportunity.

Although really enjoying painting, I realised it would be beneficial to have some understanding of basic drawing techniques. Discussing it with my husband Bob, we decided it might be good to join the evening class. We could combine my interest in art with his love of music, by dropping in on a local Musicians Open Night, after the art class. The two ladies from the exercise class decided to enrol, so at the start of the term, on a cold wet Wednesday in January, we joined an eager mixed group of aspiring sketchers.

Rhiannon was a school teacher, who also loved teaching adults. No need to ask us to be quiet or pay attention, we were all there by choice, to learn how to draw. A list of materials had been sent out, so everyone arrived with a selection of pencils, HB, 2B, 4B, an eraser, sharpener, biro and sketch book. A few people had slightly more materials, with one gentleman opening a case that contained more pencils than the rest of the group put together. Still, he could only use one a time. His selection being so wide, it added an extra thought process for him to navigate, as well as how to contain everything on his allocated table space.

Introductions around the room, confirmed a great lack of drawing skills in all but two of the group. Many had last used a pencil in school, the most artistic designs being doodles on the back pages of text books, from long forgotten subjects. Decades later, with Rhiannon's skilful guidance, the humble pencil was about to be transformed into a magic drawing tool.

The class ran from 7pm to 9pm with a short coffee break. It was surprising how cramped and tight our hands could become gripping a pencil, we certainly needed that break. Initial attempts at creating elliptical shapes, pencils in a vice like grip, juddering slowly across the paper, proved very difficult and disappointing. This is where Rhiannon started to reveal the magic. Most beginners grip the pencil using fingers and wrist to draw. By using the whole arm, a far greater range of movement can be achieved. The first lightbulb moment, why confine your pencil to your fingers when it can be an extension to your arm, giving smooth sweeping movement. With the same pencils, on the same paper, beautiful oval shapes were appearing for everyone. Why had it ever been so difficult?

With the wind howling outside and rain lashing the window panes, the atmosphere inside was cosy and congenial, as steaming mugs of coffee were brought out. Confidence boosted; the second part of the lesson looked at using these elliptical shapes to construct everyday objects. Cups and Saucers took on a new persona. Rather than admiring the delicacy of bone china, our eyes were looking for the number of oval shapes. General consensus was three for a saucer, the base, outer edge and the inner edge of the lip. At first sight the cup only appeared to have a base and top edge. However, as it was being viewed slightly from above, there was another partial oval visible due to the thickness of the china. Very early on, it became apparent that keen observation was the key to success with sketching. If you close one eye at a time you will see an object from a slightly different viewpoint. It can be helpful to look through one eye. You can try this right now, by looking at something a little way off and notice how its position changes slightly against objects further away.

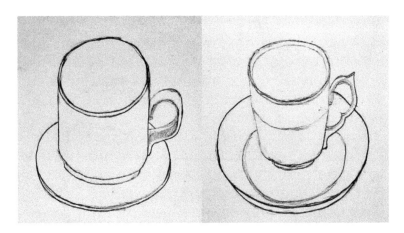

A cup and saucer seemed quite tricky; little did we know how difficult an empty jam jar would be.

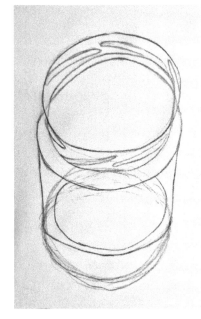

In true school teacher style, Rhiannon set us some homework. Not compulsory, but just to keep us a little active during the week, so we didn't forget all we had learnt. It was true to say, that just one lesson had been so informative.

A week flew by and it was time to meet up and continue our sketching. Having been asked to bring along any cardboard tubes we could find, these added to the growing number of pencils, erasers and paper, that needed to be packed into a suitable bag. Although only our second week, most people had amassed a lot more items, including an all important sharpener, that collected shavings. It didn't take long to realise that a basic sharpener created quite a lot of mess, or maybe we were just rather untidy. I invested in a rolled canvas pencil case, with a good range of hard and soft pencils. There were also some strange looking white paper tubes with conical ends. Not wishing to look totally clueless, I looked on line to try and find out what they were for. So simple when you know, they were for blending / smudging pencil shading. They soon became one of my favourite tools.

Everyone had completed their homework, which was to draw cups, mugs or anything that could hold a drink. We all agreed that having homework, was a great way to embed what we had started to learn.

It was very noticeable how everyone felt their attempts were just okay, keen to point out the wobbly line or area that had been erased several times. Whilst viewing each others work, they were very complimentary and picked out parts that were particularly well drawn. The lesson to be learnt from this, no matter how critical you may be of your own work, others will view it from a quite different perspective. So don't be too hard on yourself.

Our second week was all about light sources. We all knew that a shadow was made by any object that was in front of a light source. The most obvious being when a cloud passes in front of the sun, just as you have relaxed onto a sun lounger.

What we didn't know, was how much this shadow would alter depending on the exact relationship of the light to the object. This is where the cardboard tubes came into their own. Stood on the table, a shadow was instantly created. Following Rhiannon's guidance, we placed our tubes in different alignments and observed where the shadows fell. After the complexity of jam jars and cups, drawing a tube was quite easy, so we launched ourselves into the task.

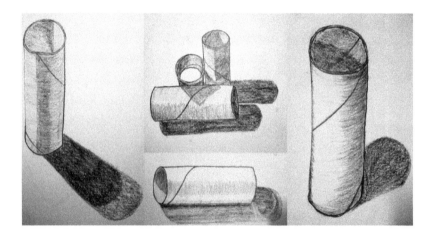

Over the weeks, there were some great fun moments, when we tried to look at an object, then draw it without looking at the paper. Rhiannon also introduced a box of very random objects, that were passed out to everyone. We then had 5 minutes to draw our object. This produced some very weird shapes where some had focused all their time on the detail of one small part. Others had completed their object, but with no detail. Swapping items, Rhiannon reduced the time by a minute until we had only one minute for our final attempt.

This speed drawing was fun, whilst teaching us the importance of observation and how the use of minimal detail, captured correctly, can be used to portray anything. These drawings took one, three and 5 minutes respectively.

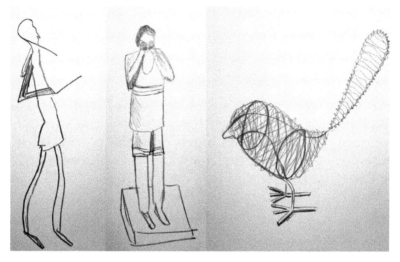

One particular topic I enjoyed was single point perspective. Being analytical, it gave me a clear understanding of how things needed to be drawn, to vanish into the distance. Guidelines can be seen vanishing behind this stack of books, to a single point.

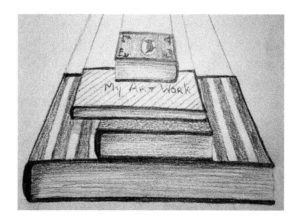

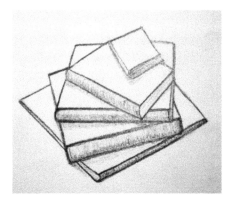

Individual guidelines to a single point were drawn for each of the spiral of books, then erased. The same process was used for this block of houses, with both streets vanishing into the distance from the corner which is closest to you.

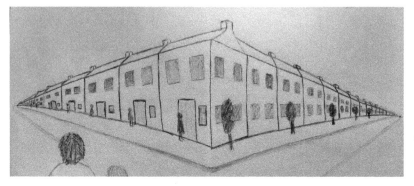

Near the middle of the course, I had my Frankenstein moment. We were looking at drawing hands. Although young at heart, reflecting years of neglect, lack of moisturiser and pampering, my hands at best could be described as having character. Providing plenty of interest, I became totally carried away and somehow extended my index finger out of all proportion to the rest of my hand. It sort of developed an extra joint, which I am happy to share, as it shows that things are often far from perfect when you first start to draw.

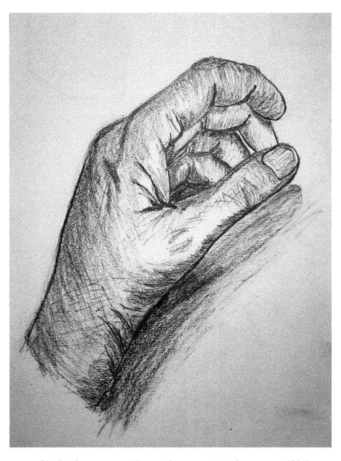

For every slightly negative element, there will be a positive part. In this instance, I was quite pleased with my thumb. It even had a hint of the scar I had gained as a child, from catching it in a swinging see-saw.

A great piece of advice, is not to immediately dismiss a sketch if you think it's not good enough. Take time to understand what didn't go exactly to plan, why it doesn't quite appear the way you intended. Then look closer, to see what you have done well. By identifying what needs to be altered and what is looking pretty okay, your next drawing will be much improved.

I drew my foot as homework and the outcome was much improved. Still a bit Frankenstein, but far closer to the real thing, reflective of an old foot, that has had surgery giving it a unique look.

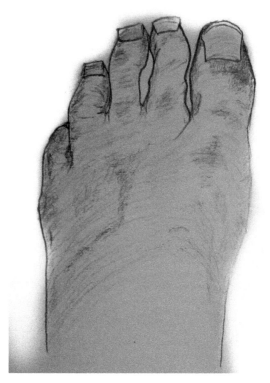

As the weeks progressed, becoming more relaxed about how to draw, our attention focused on the detail of what we were drawing. Everyone made great progress, enjoying each new topic. Diligently putting new skills into practice at home. The dreaded mention of extra homework being given out in school years, had been replaced by an eager acceptance of the techniques that could be practiced, to show an improvement by the following week. It's only when you have something to compare with, that progress can be fully acknowledged.

Towards the end of the ten weeks, with one lesson a week and practicing in our own time, everyone managed to tackle some pretty detailed still life challenges. Rhiannon was very encouraging, provided some great teaching whilst we had been studious and inquisitive pupils, keen to start learning how to draw.

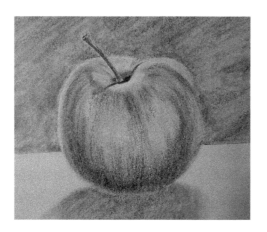

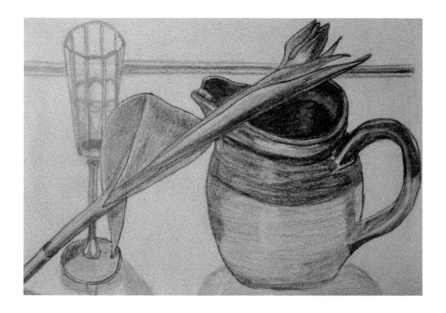

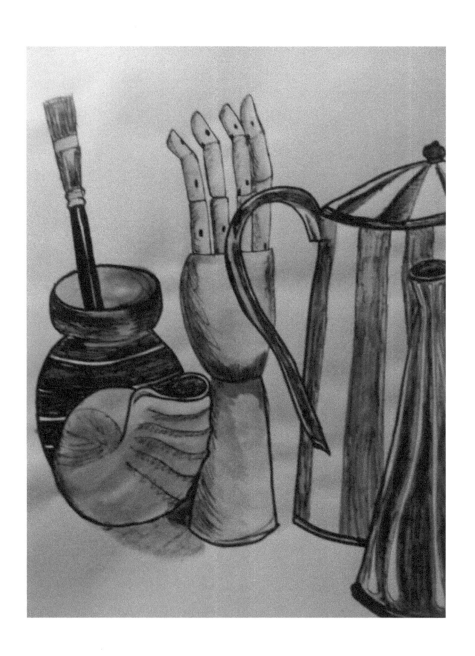

It was surprising just how much could be learnt in such a short space of time.

Bob and I were off on holiday just after the course had finished so I decided to take a sketch book, to put my new found skills into practice. It was really interesting looking at plants and buildings with new "artists eyes". Rather than reading books, spending relaxation time drawing all sorts of interesting things. Being mindful that shadows would alter as the sun moved during the day. With my love of botanical art, observing the different leaf shapes and structural patterns of the many exotic plants, became a passion.

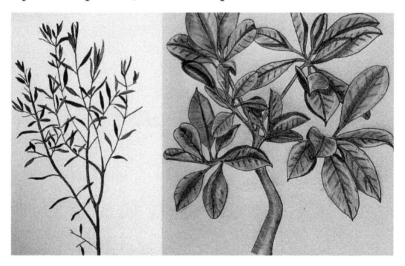

Most artists are known for a particular style of work, be it rolling landscapes, captivating portraits or great wall murals. If you start your art for pleasure, you are not governed by any style, so can enjoy the freedom of painting and drawing anything that captures your imagination. This was how I spent one sunny afternoon drawing lots of little houses. The view was so pretty, with whitewashed buildings bathed in sunlight against a beautiful blue sky. With only a few pencils and markers, I set about capturing the scene.

Remembering the lesson on single point perspective, attempting to graduate the size of the buildings as they became more distant. The result was a little wonky in places, but the overall drawing captured the essence of the scene. It had also given me opportunity to gaze repeatedly at all the detail, which captured the view in my mind. Although we all seek perfection, our best effort can be a very good goal. Banishing my critical voice, this drawing holds so many happy memories. Looking at it, I can feel the warmth of the day, hear the birds and insects, transported back to the relaxing time spent on holiday with a sketchbook.

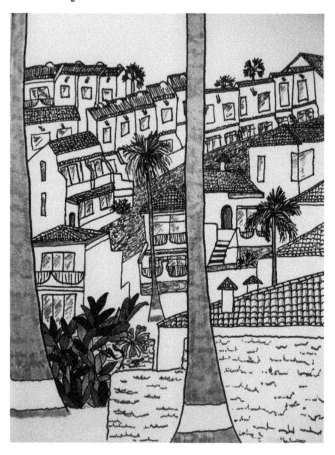

Having decided early on that portraits and body parts were not for me, sketching the holiday street scene, opened up a door to buildings and architecture. With the National Trust, many interesting days had been spent walking through gardens and enjoying the history, of magnificent old buildings. With an artistic eye, the architecture and design opened up a whole new sketching opportunity. Returning home, keen to continue my new interest in drawing buildings, I visited Dyffryn Gardens, where I had first seen Debbie's beautiful botanical art. This time I was there to soak up the detail of the exterior of the building. Sketchbook and pencils packed, what may have seemed a daunting task, was actually an exciting opportunity. How fortunate to have such a great building so close to home to practice my drawing.

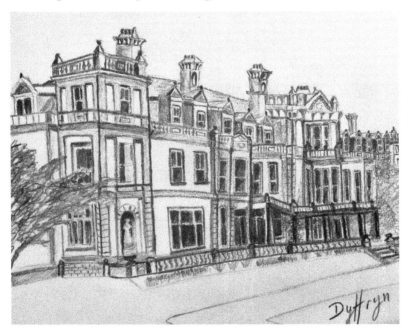

Dyffryn pencil sketch

Like the finger with the extra joint, this drawing has a slightly odd angle in the middle of the ground floor. But does it matter? Knowing it's there, is part of learning by doing. Always view your art so that slight flaws create opportunities to improve. At the same time celebrate all the bits that went well. Remembering the single point perspective from Rhiannon, I managed to show that the left of the building was closer and the view was clearly from a slight angle, not directly face on.

Another local building of interest was Insole Court, where I had enjoyed winter months at my sketching night class. Returning during the day, it was a delightful and challenging building to continue improving my sketching skills.

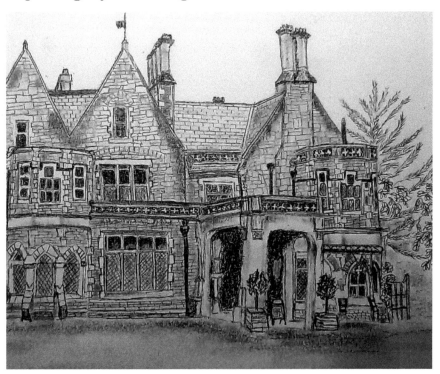

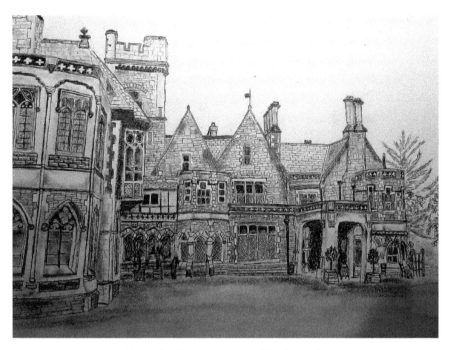

Insole Court pencil sketch.

If in doubt about your drawing, reflect on my two tea cup sketches that have led me to draw two Mansions. Over time, small steps will lead to a great improvement in your art.

Chapter 4
Watercolour Weekend

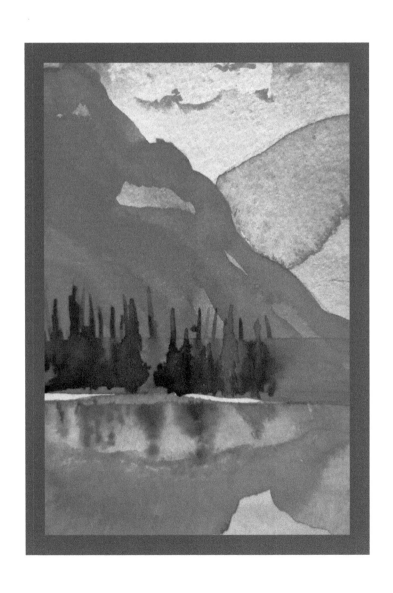

Over the past two years, Rachel and I had spent some mum and daughter time visiting London. With a very well-planned itinerary, show tickets booked and places grouped daily, for ease of travel. These trips had run like clockwork, with some slightly more unusual locations added, to make our stay interesting. Notably, a visit to Dennis Servers House, at 18 Folegate Street, which was unlike any other tour that we had ever encountered.

Visiting during the twilight hours, the Georgian Terraced house was only lit with candles. There were ten rooms to view, each was a time capsule, reflecting life in the 18th and 19th centuries. The house contents portrayed a fictional family of Huguenot silk weavers. Abandoned like the Marie Celeste, there were partly eaten meals on the table, half empty glasses and coats hung in the hallway. One rule to be strictly adhered to, was silence. No one was allowed to talk, only walk through the rooms, looking at a vast number of intriguing objects, whilst reading small cards outlining the history of the room. The candles flickered and a coach and horses could be heard pulling up outside. Draughts could be felt and distant conversation heard from rooms across the hallway. Entering the master bedroom, there was a faint aroma of cloves and oranges, then shattering the silence a large clock in the hall struck the hour. Spending time exploring in silence and being able to soak up the atmosphere, was a truly magical experience.

However, our mum and daughter time this year was to be magical in a much different way. Having enjoyed our taster of Botanical Art classes, we were keen to try a far more loose and free way of painting. So, we were off to Mapledurham for our long weekend.

Setting out early to make the most of our time away, I drove the short distance to pick up Rachel and we headed off. One of the few areas of disagreement between mother and daughter was the use of a Sat Nav. Not wishing to start our adventure with any animosity, settling behind the wheel, I allowed Rachels new iPhone to confidently issue eloquent instructions. "At the roundabout, take the third exit and continue on Oxford Road". Our journey should have been around two hours, but half way the eloquent voice just stopped. There were no guiding words to allow us to "reach our destination". Pulling into a very unfamiliar service station, a trusty map was retrieved from the boot. We had somehow ended up in the Cotswolds instead of being at our first destination of the day, Basildon Park. After a strong coffee, whilst pouring over the well-worn and folded map, we were no longer lost, just slightly off course, well 100 miles actually.

Eventually the gates of Basildon Park were in sight, but there were only a handful of cars in the parking area. By now the temperature had dropped considerably even for February. Wrapping up with scarves and gloves, approaching the entrance, fortunately the National Trust staff were still in attendance, pondering on the lack of visitors, due to the weather. Inside was stunning, like Dennis Servers house only on very grand scale. With next to no visitors, we had room after room with just the two of us, taking in the splendour of the decor and furnishings. A lot of the artworks were huge and very detailed, so much to take in. Having tried painting botanical art, we now appreciated the skill of the artists who had painted all of these landscapes, still life images and family portraits. With the place almost to ourselves, there was plenty of time to take in all the intricate details woven into each room.

Dating back to 1806, the highlight of the visit was the India – inspired Zuber wallpaper.

This was exotic opulence at its greatest. Mahouts with their bejewelled elephants, transporting Princes. Bold colours used for exotic foliage along with exquisite reflections of temples rising up in the centre of lakes. Once again, with only minimal experience of painting, we were still very much able to appreciate how extraordinary this Indian mural wallpaper was.

Venturing out into the vast grounds, the cold air wrapped its fingers around us, causing us to stiffen and shiver. With hands deep in pockets and shoulders hunched, we set out to explore the park. It was bleak and exposed, a dull grey sky and dark woods in the distance. There were several detailed walks up to five miles, however we decided to take the shortest option. Sufficient to appreciate the huge age-old trees and expansive gardens, extending to fields and surrounding woodland. It was quite eerie passing only two other people on the entire circuit.

Glad to reach the car, a decision had to be made on whether to visit Beale Park. Fortunately, our love of exploring new places and the chance to see some Peacocks won over the now biting cold. After all, it was only just down the road and then it wouldn't be far to our accommodation.

There were possibly twenty people in the whole park. Being the only people on the little railway, we could see all around us, gaining a good idea of the areas we would like to see more of and those that could be left. With almost exclusive viewing, we were able to observe the Alpacas and Meerkats at close quarters. Taking lots of photos, so that we could later use them for drawings and paintings.

We almost forgot the cold wrapped around us, as we took multiple shots of ring-tailed lemurs with their enquiring eyes. It was going to be fun trying to capture their poses on paper.

Having started to paint, we had developed a greater sense of observation, enjoying pointing out different aspects to each other. Previously, we would have just looked and thought they were cute, not appreciating their sudden statue like pause, as they heard a noise, or the way their noses were raised in the air and their ringed tails slowly curled. The highlight of Beale Park, was following the free roaming Peacocks. Without a visitor in sight, we were able to slowly manoeuvre into an advantageous position, taking some stunning photos of these magnificent birds. There was still just enough weak sunlight, to show off their multiple shades of blue and green plumage. It would certainly be challenging to try creating these, mixing different colours on a pallet. At this point, we knew there were so many different colours with very exotic names, but what really mattered was how we chose to interpret what we saw. Only we would know if our chosen peacock was a deep Prussian Blue with a hint of Cobalt Green. Art is so unique to the artist, that we could have created a Sky Blue and Gold peacock. A truth always to be remembered, artistic licence allows for a great freedom of creativity.

With the light fading and our faces pinched with the cold, we left the beautiful birds, animals and water gardens, in search of Mapledurham. As we drove, any hint of urbanisation was left behind, as we followed the winding country roads. Finally arriving at our little B&B. There had been limited accommodation in such a rural area and we were glad to have booked into somewhere close to the art studio.

Our rooms were really warm and welcoming, although a little dated, which added to the quaint rural charm. After such a busy day, we were really looking forward to our dinner reservation. Having changed into fresh clothes, looking outside, it had become pitch dark.

Used to city life, we decided not to venture out walking on an unlit road. Driving a few hundred yards, on the opposite side of the road, the old thatched pub was the only building in sight. What better way to end the day, with a roaring fire and excellent food. Our art adventure had certainly begun.

Rising early the next morning, breakfast was skipped, to ensure plenty of time to navigate the narrow country lanes, to reach the art studio. Uphill and down dale revealed a quaint little hamlet, with beautiful thatched cottages and an old church. The art studio, a barn conversion, was nestled next to the church, with a life size black and white cow covered in red spots, taking pride of place in the car park. No need to worry that we had found the right place.

Liz our teacher, greeted us with a bright smile and led the way to the upstairs chill out area. Wow, there were paintings everywhere. Large ones, small ones, animals, birds, buildings, flowers, almost too much to take in. Large sofas with comfy cushions beckoned, with all manner of art books arrayed on two equally large coffee tables.

There were only three other participants, with introductions easily made, we relaxed with a coffee as Liz explained the format of the weekend. No one had any great artistic background, so we were pretty much at ease with one another and hugely excited about entering a real art studio.

Making our way down the rear staircase, we entered a large open studio, with a high, light oak, beamed ceiling. Windows ran around two sides, allowing the natural daylight to flood in.

It was like an Artists version of Aladdin's cave. Easels propped against the wall, all sizes of paint brushes, pallets full of watercolours, paper, tissues, water sprays, pencils, loads of kitchen roll for the odd spill and most important, a row of aprons on wooden pegs, baptised with real paint splodges. We were now apprentice artists, with our own work spaces set up all ready to be used.

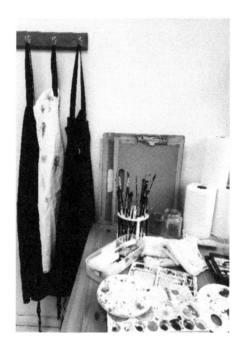

Liz really put everyone at ease, starting off with a lot of bold squiggles and circles on a large piece of paper. We then swept lines of different colours over the top, to understand which colours were opaque and which were transparent.

All became so clear, just using the paints rather than reading some lengthy guide on the characteristics of watercolours.

By the first coffee break, five pieces of paper had been adorned with a multitude of brightly coloured falling feathers. All different, each reflecting the colour choices of their creator, with a few tentative attempts at feathers followed by large sweeping colourful plumes, as confidence grew. Mutual admiration of the best feathers, was balanced with mutual appreciation of the initial hesitant strokes, that hadn't quite flowed. General consensus, it all boiled down to having the confidence to just give it a try.

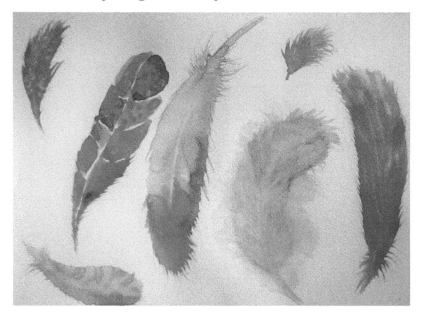

A strong connection having been established between the five group members; all were eager to see what was coming next. Liz demonstrated a beautiful scene, with trees reflected on the edge of a lake, distant mountains echoed in the deep water and light clouds drifting by. This was created using one tube of blue watercolour paint. It looked so perfect, and seemed to be way beyond everyone's capabilities. Yet, looking back at the feathers, a certain level of bravado crept into the group, as different amounts of water were added to create several shades of blue. Despite a few over saturated areas and slightly strange shaped shadows, five blue landscapes began to emerge on the blank sheets of paper. With the odd intake of breath, as the paint decided to take its own path, the mountains grew and the water began to show reflections of distant pine trees.

They say time flies when you are having fun. In this case, time flew as paint met paper and magically conjured up five mountain scenes. Each very different with a unique style all of its own.

Everyone found interesting elements in each other's work, but also managed to find fault with elements of their own painting. This was where Liz stepped in, with some beautiful examples of where things had possibly not gone as expected with her own work. Acknowledging that watercolour has a will of its own, any irregularities were just by chance, so only the artist would know. Looking at her examples, we had to agree, particularly when she pointed out some cauliflowers. No, we hadn't switched to still life fruit and vegetables, this was apparently a well-known technical term, in watercolour circles. It describes a bloom, shaped rather like a cauliflower, that appears when very wet paint has been introduced to a not quite dry area.

Some artists encourage it, to add texture and character, perfect for mottled foliage in uneven light. With the reason for cauliflowers now understood, in future, they could possibly be avoided, created, or just calmly accepted as part of painting in watercolour.

With new found knowledge, having achieved so much in one morning, there was plenty to talk about over a light lunch, in the chill out area.

The afternoon brought a new technique into play, the use of masking fluid, to create a tree abundant in cherry blossom. We were each given a reference picture and a blank sheet of paper. Liz demonstrated the process with one critical warning, never to use a good brush. Rather like latex glue, the fluid was dabbed randomly over the paper, where the blossom was to be seen. Mainly on the tree with some petals floating in the breeze or fallen to the ground. Once dry, it acted as a barrier to any paint. Various shades of blue were confidently transformed into a delicate sky, with greens mixed and merged, to convey an area of grass.

This process couldn't be rushed, the masking fluid needed to be dry, then the layers of blue and green paint needed to dry. What a good opportunity to set our work aside, enjoy another coffee, and ask a whole host of questions. Liz was our personal Art Guru, full of knowledge and great at explaining things in a way that we could understand. By the end of the break, any feelings of unease, from exposing our lack of knowledge, had been firmly dismissed. We were all there to enjoy learning as much as possible, thriving on the experience.

There was growing anticipation, to execute the finishing steps, to reveal our cherry blossom pictures. All quietly confident we could actually get there.

Carefully rolling away the masking fluid, lots of little white marks were revealed. To Transform them into a tree, we added a dark brown twisted trunk. With lower branches visible, as they grew upwards, less could be seen, the tiniest twigs vanishing into the blossom.

Adding these strong brown brush strokes, transformed our random white marks, into a tree. The final touches, a long shadow stretching out beneath the tree and some delicate pink shading, randomly scattered over the white blossom. Now we were really starting to feel like artists. Success was in the air, smiles on faces, paint mostly on paper, with the odd stray splodge on our aprons.

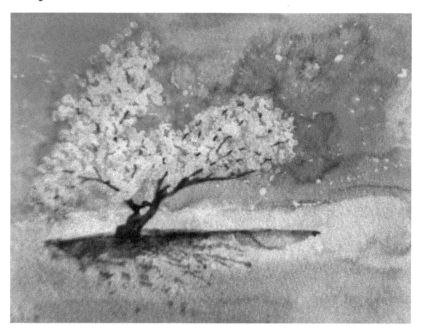

What a beautiful day, first feathers then a mountain scene finishing up with a beautiful cherry tree. Far more than we had ever imagined we capable of doing.

Time to pack up, carefully wash brushes, wipe tables, empty water jars, aprons on pegs, leaving everything neat and tidy for the next day.

Two of our group lived locally, but the third had travelled early in the morning and was staying at our B&B. We managed to alter our evening meal booking, so we could dine together.

There was a great sense of camaraderie, as we re-lived the events of the day, over a well-deserved meal. Exotic deserts rewarded our busy day, as the re-telling of Liz's many anecdotes, brought a jovial air to the conversation. How lucky we were to have found art, being bold enough to step out of our comfort zones and search for ways to improve our painting. By doing this, we had found an excellent teacher, met some very interesting and likeminded people. Learning so much, by just having a go at painting something different.

Day two was like an old friend's reunion. Steaming coffee mugs warming our hands, we sat on the large sofas discussing the merits of all the paintings around the room. There were so many, hanging on the walls, leaning against the stair rail and suspended from the beams. Chickens, cows, goats, otters, penguins, flowers, landscapes, castles, all manner of art. How wonderful that someone with such a talent, was also blessed with the ability to put us at ease and deliver such enjoyable coaching.

Entering our studio, taking our aprons from their pegs, we filled our water jars and sat in our places. Relaxed and at ease we listened to Liz outline the day. This was our day to be creative, we would be shown some more techniques for backgrounds and silhouettes, then be allowed to paint anything!

Being slightly cautious, I chose to do a turquoise humming bird on a wet in wet background. Having learnt that this technique required the background area to be dampened, then wet colours introduced, to blend into each other. Confident that the water would do its own thing, whilst I sat back and watched. The waiting was important, not to keep introducing more colour and risking a cauliflower. Blue and yellow blended to create subtle shades of green, to complement my turquoise bird silhouette.

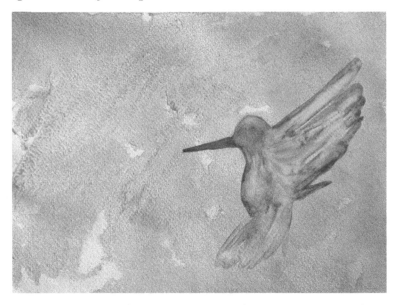

Rachel was very adventurous, with a wet in wet sky incorporating five colours, providing a fantasy backdrop for a camel on top of a high sand dune. The colours blended beautifully and dried well. Being a little more complex than the rest of the group, she was slightly later starting her camel silhouette. Then disaster struck, a cauliflower began to bloom on the hump of her multicoloured camel. At the precise moment Rachel let out a disheartened groan, everyone else happened to be painting in a state of silent concentration.

Suddenly all eyes were upon her, what had happened to her beautiful Arabian Night fantasy.

Liz calmly assessed the damage and suggested that rather than try to disguise it, a further cauliflower should be encouraged. This gave the impression of two paniers on the camel's hump, creating curiosity. What treasure was this lone camel carrying across the desert. Disaster averted, everyone marvelled at the realisation, this was exactly what Liz had said the previous day.

No one but the artist knows what should or shouldn't be in the painting. A very important lesson, for anyone deciding to take up art.

This not only applies to any mistakes you feel you have made. Rachel chose to depict her camel in a range of colours, including blue and pink. It is very doubtful that a blue camel has ever existed, but for a painting it is totally acceptable, because art is all about personal interpretation.

The outline shape clearly registers with us that this is a camel. The fact that the colours are not as we expect them to be, makes us more interested in looking at the picture.

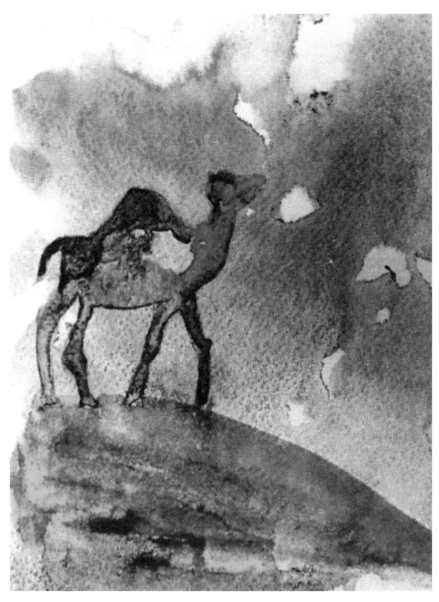

Camel by Rachel Trusler

Our final afternoon was spent painting from a favourite picture, we had been asked to take with us. Having a sweet tooth and loving chocolate cakes, I'd selected a picture of some cupcakes, made for afternoon tea, presented on a cake stand. Thinking this would be far easier than a landscape or animal.

With a far greater appreciation of the nature of watercolour and the techniques used to enhance it, several key areas sprang to mind. The tiered plates needed to be in proportion, with the upper casting a shadow beneath it. The central brass rod needed to look cylindrical whilst reflecting the light. The dark chocolate coatings needed to shine, whilst the white chocolate was actually cream, enhancing the 3D milk chocolate hearts decorating them.

The very fact that I was thinking along these lines, showed a much-improved ability, to observe colour and detail when creating a piece of art. Even the paper cake cases came with light and shade, a cylindrical appearance and challenging little concertina edges, blending into the chocolate toppings. Everything comes with practice, this was an opportunity to recognise what was needed, seek advice and guidance then give it a try.

The biggest step is the first brush stroke, once in place, other brush marks then fall into place. It's not about perfection, your creativity is your key to enjoying art.

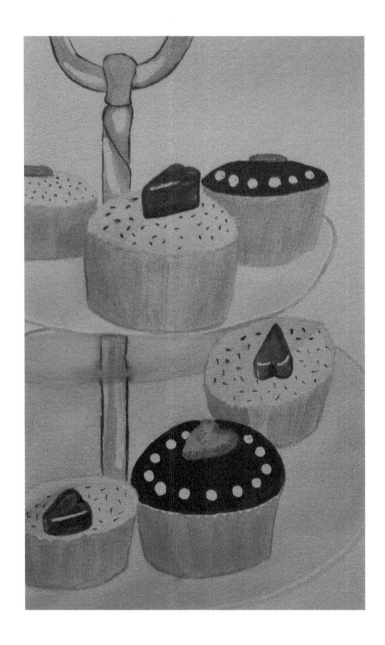

It can be quite difficult to paint something in a realistic way, with your art becoming almost like a photo image. However, this challenge is really good for improving your attention to detail.

Rachel had chosen a pet rabbit, deciding to focus on his face and ears, whilst being very bold and using pink, blue and yellow to portray his character. One ear stood upright whilst the other flopped sideways. The wet in wet technique worked beautifully with her three colours, subtly merging into shades of lilac and green. Ensuring there were white highlights in the deep blue eyes, brought the painting of Gus to life. This happy bunny, was staring straight out from the page, ready to hop forward at any moment. So, what if one cheek was slightly larger than the other, he had probably just pulled a carrot and was trying to look innocent of the deed.

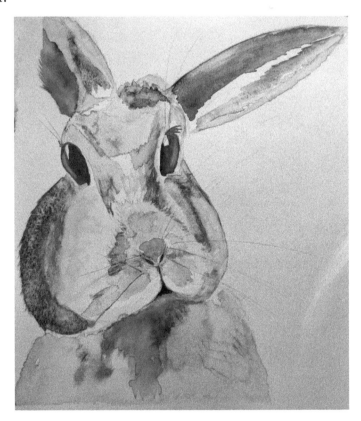

Bunny by Rachel Trusler

Lining up for a group photo, in front of the red spotted cow, holding our paintings, happiness shone from smiling faces. It had been a brilliant two days, no one ever felt worried about their lack of experience. We were all a little sad leaving our studio and our chill out area. For one weekend we had allowed our inner artist to escape into the magical world of art.

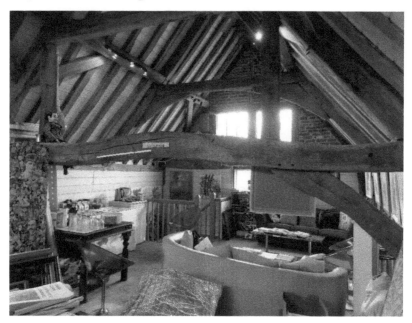

Learning by doing, we could return home and repeat the processes with confidence, as we had all created some very respectable pieces of artwork over the two days.

It's never too late to start your art journey and there are so many people like Liz, who really enjoy sharing their skills.

What a great mum and daughter weekend. Previous London trips had been very enjoyable, this experience went to the next level, enabling us to share our inner creativity.

Driving home, there was a glorious glowing sunset. The perfect end to a perfect experience. Rachel took some impromptu photos, with great artistic potential. A dark motorway with dotted white headlights, a magnificent orange glowing sky, blending to yellow, then deep blue, with the silhouette of electric pylons vanishing into the distance.

Previously acknowledged as a lovely sunset, this scene was now so much more. Wet in wet with merging colours, tiny headlights left to shine white, using masking fluid, finished off with architectural shapes, suggesting pylons silhouetted against the sunset.

Once ignited, the creativity just grows.

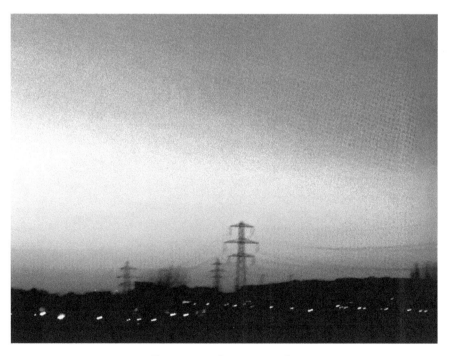

Sunset photograph

With many new techniques and tips, it was exciting to return home and try them out. The first painting on my mind was to try and capture the motorway sunset. Using the masking fluid for the stream of car headlights. Experimenting with very wet paper, to blend the sunset colours and to capture the essence of a wonderful weekend.

Courses like this can really boost your confidence, Enabling you to enjoy time with likeminded people, who are equally excited about learning to paint.

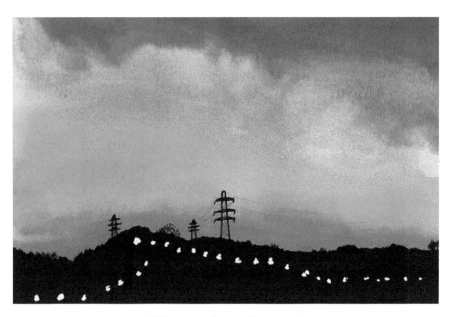

Watercolour Sunset

Chapter 5
Loose Florals

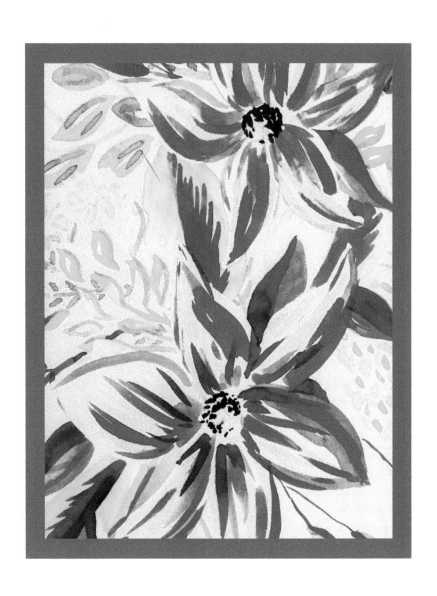

Leaving the motorway to drive along pleasant country roads, I felt an air of excitement, as my destination was only a few miles away. Pretty soon, I turned into the main entrance and parked in the shade of a large horse chestnut tree. The grand Victorian building had been beautifully restored and the main entrance was very impressive. From the reception desk, a very young girl with a shock of bright pink highlights, directed me to the Lilac room. As I opened the door, a shaft of light shone through the wide bay window, picking out the beautiful vases of fresh flowers, placed on the large dining table. Another young lady welcomed me to the Floral Art Day and offered refreshments. This provided time to admire the beautiful décor, whilst becoming acquainted with the other participants. At this point I was feeling relaxed and eager to make a start.

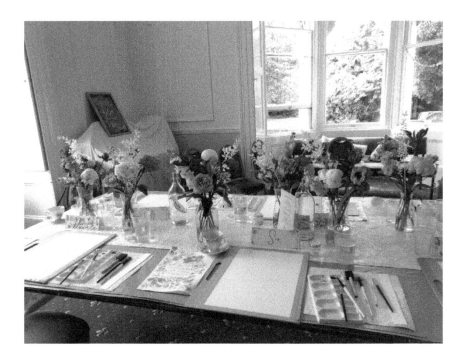

We were invited to take our seats behind hand painted floral place cards. Introductions began at the far end of the table, with a sportswear designer, who had always wanted to try floral art with inks. Then a lady in her forties with a degree in Fine Arts, wanting to refresh her skills. To my left, a niche shop owner specialising in Gothic Art creations. Suddenly everyone is looking at me. Heart racing, I took a deep breath and described myself as retired, with no art background, looking forward to the day. My inner voice reminding me, if all else fails, remain calm. To my right, a mother and daughter, on a break from running their ceramics business. Completing the group, were two Art college friends, enjoying a creative reunion. All lovely ladies, what if a few of them were even younger than my daughter, my internal panic attack was that each of them had a profession in art. A second insecurity followed close behind. Why weren't we going to use watercolours? By now, I was anything but relaxed and certainly not ready to start creating a floral masterpiece with ink.

When I arrived at the venue, chatting with these ladies, over light refreshments, I initially felt quite comfortable in their company. With exchanges of miles travelled, beautiful weather, partners left to fend for themselves and enthusiasm for the day, we appeared to be very much on a level playing field. After the formal introductions, I had suddenly felt very much out of my depth, with everyone else having professional artistic backgrounds. Luckily our teacher Jess, was so pleasant telling us about the format of the day, that I decided to give it my best shot. The warm up was brilliant and could easily have been created with me in mind. Jess gave a quick demonstration of how to paint and make marks with ink.

We were asked to stand up and look at the flowers in front of us. Using just blue ink and a large brush we had to outline the largest flower shapes, on the paper in front of us. Rather like musical chairs, we then had to stop, put our brushes down and move one place to the left. This time we picked up the paint brushes and added in the smaller shapes. Stems and leaves were added in the same way. By the end, I had painted on 5 different pictures. My shaky contribution blended in with everyone else's and the final artworks looked quite presentable. All without any sketched outlines, just by looking at the flowers and suggesting the shapes with a loose brushstroke.

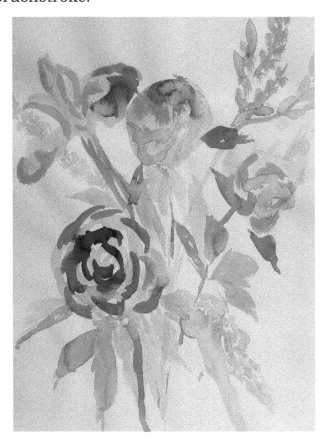

By mid morning, I had learnt how to use a "sponge stick" as well as some rather large paint brushes. With botanical art, some of the brushes were tiny going down to a double zero. The smallest size Jess used was a size 8, moving up to size 12. There was no way these could be gripped like a biro, so I was forced to throw caution to the wind and hold the brush far higher up. Surprisingly, this provided a much more fluid movement, so keeping the flowers loose. Making me think back to my canal art, when I first held the brush in a vice like grip, then learnt to relax into sweeping ticks. It felt quite nice to put brush to paper, without having to follow pencil lines. Giving a lot more freedom to move the brush around, without fear of spoiling the piece.

Although we all had chrysanthemums, peonies and stocks, each vase of flowers was an individual arrangement. They also looked quite different, depending on whether you sat down, looking at eye level, or stood up and looked down on the blooms. It was a totally different painting experience, standing up. To my surprise, a couple of the other ladies also hadn't actually tried it before.

Whilst waiting for our work to dry, there was an opportunity to have a morning coffee with homemade cakes, made by the ladies running the venue. Jess put out a lot of her artwork and we all looked in awe. They were so perfectly vibrant and alive. Taking part in the warm up exercise had removed my insecurities and I found myself happily discussing loose floral art with the rest of the group. I was beginning to realise just how much respect artists have, for fellow artists. Jess was a Printed Textile Designer and Artist, with designs available in a number of well-known high street stores at home and overseas.

Initially attracted to her work through Instagram, I hadn't really realised how accomplished she was. Probably just as well, because I was still lacking confidence and may not have booked her floral art day. With hindsight, my advice, would be to just follow your heart. If you want to paint anything, just go for it. No one is born holding a paintbrush, so everyone has to make that initial brushstroke. Some people start early, but others like me start quite late on in life. This does give you the advantage of patience, also an understanding that things are not always perfect first time.

Coffee over, Jess talked about her painting process. Her work is so bright and vibrant because there is a lot of white left untouched. A particular process is needed to achieve this, which is how I first fell in love with Pebeo masking fluid. Its light blue tint meant it was really easy to see on the paper. After using white masking fluid, this was so much better. Although it still messed up brushes. Should you ever use masking fluid, never use a good brush, as it's a bit like PVA glue and even when rinsed off immediately, still leaves residue over time. Its purpose is to protect areas of paper that need to stay white, whilst colours are being applied all around. Once peeled off, it's like a reverse silhouette.

Jess used large sheets of paper, attached to firm MDF or plywood boards, with gummed brown tape. This was where the mystery of stretching paper was revealed. By wetting the paper with clean water and taping it to a firm board, it tightens as it dries. Enabling a smooth uniform background to be painted, it is also much less likely to cockle when dampened and paint applied. Luckily Jess had previously stretched some paper for us to use, as it can be quite a time consuming process.

Unused to such large A2 (420 x 594 mm) sheets of paper and without an art studio at home, space was going to be rather limited for lots of boards to be left drying with stretched paper.

I have since realised that stretching paper is a very personal thing. Some artists swear by it and others wouldn't dream of doing it. Those that do, have so many different techniques; saturating the paper and removing the residue with kitchen roll, or applying water with a spray. My advice is not to get hung up with stretching. Give it a try, but decide for yourself, what suits you best. I like blocks of paper which are glued together on all 4 edges, with a small gap left usually at the top. The paper stays pretty flat and can be separated from the block once complete, by inserting a thin knife into the gap and running it around the edges. Saves a lot on stretching space and time.

Our first task was to look at the vases of flowers and use masking fluid to put a couple of large flower shapes onto our paper. This needed to become fully dry, so we used the time to select our ink colours. Carefully pouring pinks, blues and yellows into our hollowed pallets. We were using water-based inks which could be lifted out with bleach once dry, to create highlights and contrast. The alternative was Acrylic Ink, which could not be lightened in this way.

With the masking fluid dry, it was time to apply a light turquoise background. I had always found this quite difficult with watercolour paint, creating unwanted streaks and the dreaded cauliflowers. Inks were so different, much stronger pigment and a very fluid watery consistency. At last, an opportunity to really see what the strange sponge wedges on sticks could do. Much to my surprise, the ink flowed smoothly across the page guided by the sponge.

The secret was to keep moving back and forth starting at the top, keeping a wet edge. It dried like magic into a smooth uniform background, looking as if I had exchanged my white paper for a sheet of coloured paper. If I learnt nothing more that day, it would have been well worth attending, just for creating my first almost perfect background.

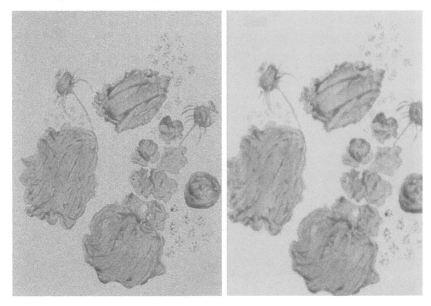

Fortunately, there were some basic similarities with watercolours and watercolour ink. The most important was working from light to dark. When using Acrylics for Canal Art, the process was mainly from dark to light. It had taken quite a bit of adjusting to learn to paint with watercolour. Fortunately, this knowledge would really help with using inks, causing earlier anxieties to further melt away.

With the Pebeo applied and the background coloured, the next step was to put in some background foliage.

Following this new process, a picture was beginning to emerge. With foliage complete, the Pebeo was carefully removed to reveal white paper.

The final step was to add in the main flowers, taking care not to cover too much of the white paper. This was by far the hardest part. On my first Loose Floral work, the flowers to the right were over coloured and insufficient white left exposed. The blooms to the left had a lot more white left exposed, but the colours were too pale, so were overpowered by the background. Yet I was really pleased, I understood the process. Due to the excellent tuition from Jess, I knew what improvements to make for my next attempt.

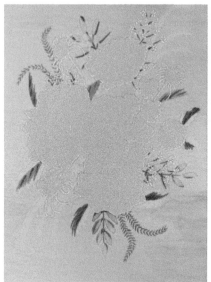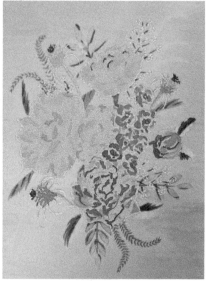

The day that had started so well, but then became shadowed with doubt and nerves during the introductions, had swung right around by the end of the morning session.

Lunch was taken sitting in the gardens, marvelling at the creative skills we had experienced during the morning session. The day was being run as two stand alone sessions, so some of the ladies left at this point. Having travelled a fair distance, it had made sense to book the afternoon session as well. With such mixed emotions throughout the morning, I was now eager to get started and build on my earlier learning. What a difference a little knowledge and confidence can make. Settling into the afternoon session, the new people once again had a wealth of artistic background. Having gained so much during the morning, when it was time to introduce myself, a timid amateur had been replaced by an excited, enthusiastic, emerging artist.

Booking two sessions was a brilliant way to reinforce the new processes and start to relax. These tutorials were only run at this location, a few times during the year, so there wasn't an option to pop back in a week or so to refresh my learning. The saying "practice makes perfect" may be a step too far, but practicing painting, certainly leads to improvement. The format of the afternoon was almost a rerun of the morning, but this time rather than worrying that I was out of my depth, I soaked up all the coaching and really enjoyed myself. If you ever feel out of your comfort zone, just look at it from a different perspective, as an opportunity to learn something new. After my day with Jess, I often look back to remind myself how much I learnt. Experience can only be gained by being bold enough to give things a try and learn by doing.

That afternoon, I focused on producing my first two Floral Masterpieces. Maybe not other peoples view of a masterpiece, but for me they were a great achievement, setting me off on another artistic pathway.

I couldn't wait to order some sponge sticks, inks and blue Pebeo!

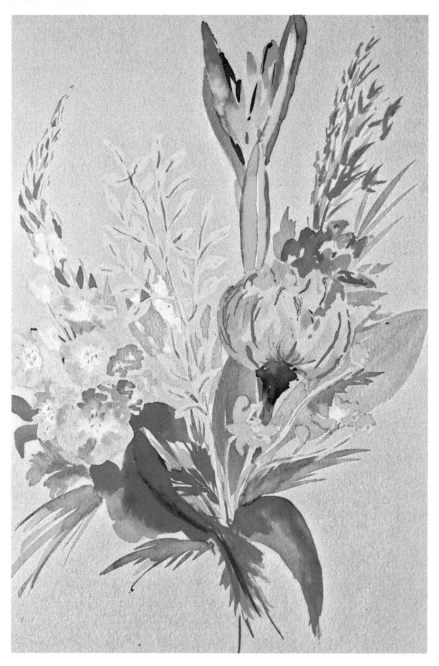

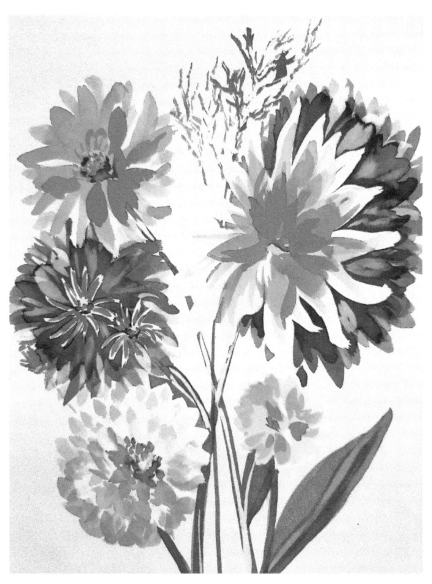

That day I met Shiree, an artist from Devon. We got on really well, both enjoying the very expressive and loose style that Jess was teaching us. When another Floral Art course was advertised several months later, we both messaged each other to sign up.

Having had time to practice using inks and developing a looser style, it was perfect timing to progress our learning. Second time around, I was relaxed, proud to say I had started art quite late in life and certainly enjoyed the day with Jess and Shiree.

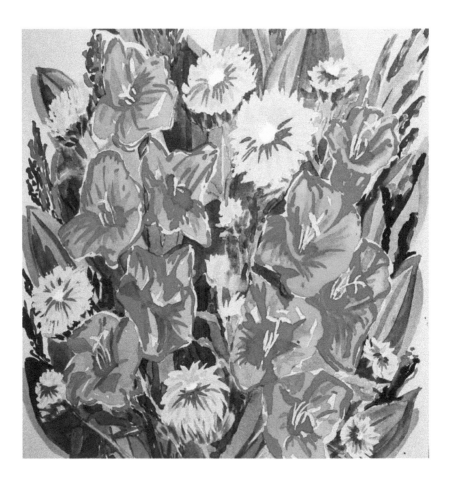

Returning home, it was great fun to try out all the new techniques that Jess had taught us.

Chapter 6
What's Out There

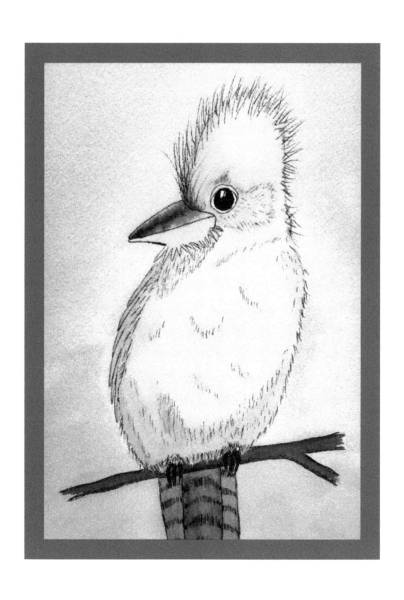

Having been introduced to different styles of art, you may well be wondering what options are available for finding some guidance. My initial venture into painting canal art roses was very much self-taught, through observation and experimenting. Managing to source only one book on Traditional Canal Art, it provided some ideas for painting, although mainly focused on the history of canal art, with pictures of coal scuttles and ornate doors. The coal scuttles were mainly on a black background with a lot of decorative borders as well as roses. The door panels often had castles, which were a key part of the traditional way of decorating barges. Neither quite fitted what I had in mind for our little narrowboat.

Basic deduction suggested watercolours would not be waterproof or bold enough, oil paints would probably take a long time to dry, so I opted for acrylic paints. Chapter 1 confirms this was a very hit and miss learning process, where patience and determination eventually took me over the finish line.

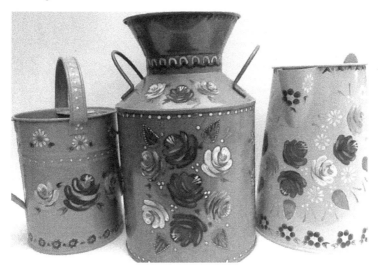

Thankfully, you do not have to meander along such a haphazard path. Having found so many different learning options, ranging from zero cost to hundreds of pounds, they are here for you to see. Learning timescales can range from ten minutes, one hour or one day, through to weekends and full term courses. Remember, when you are painting or drawing for your own enjoyment, there are no hard and fast rules. For me it was very beneficial taking an evening class in drawing, but if you have some skills learnt in school that could be rekindled, then learning to sketch may not be so important to you. Just starting to sketch everyday objects may be enough to set you off in the right direction, reviving your skills.

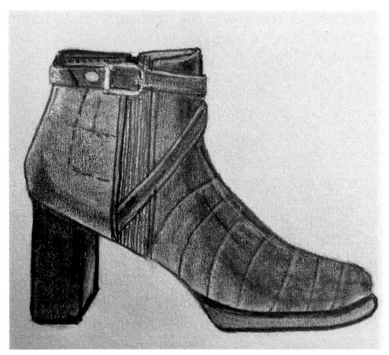

With today's technology, one of the easiest places to find anything is online. By just typing into Google "You Tube watercolour tutorials" a vast number of free tutorials appear. These usually range from five minutes to an hour. It's often best to narrow your search to flowers, animals, buildings, landscapes or whatever you feel like trying. As with everything, there are some excellent tutorials whilst others can be lacking in content or poorly produced. However, as they are free, there is nothing lost by looking. Some professional artists post ten minute tips and taster lessons, to encourage you to purchase tutorials, if you like their style. The only word of caution is not to believe everything you are told. Often people get into doing something a particular way, to the extent that they imply it is the only way. Always remember there are no boundaries to your art, because it belongs to you. If you choose to take a Fine Arts Degree, then you need to adhere to the course criteria, but to paint for pleasure you are in control of what you choose to do.

There are some techniques and processes that can prove very helpful. As I found during Loose Florals, blue Pebeo masking fluid was so much easier to use than white masking fluid. A very good source of information online is from the paint and material suppliers. Windsor & Newton have a range of tutorials so you are able to see how their colours and paints can be used. Some large art suppliers such as Cass Art and Jacksons Art also have professional tutorials available on You Tube or from their websites. Ken Bromley Art Supplies has a blog with free tutorials and an art materials guide. Derwent even have a short tutorial just on Eraser Techniques! Once you start looking, the choice of free material online is almost endless.

Be a little selective, remember your main objective is to start your art, not sit watching endless tutorials and becoming overwhelmed. I've been there on your behalf, creating a mass of spreadsheets and lots of notes thinking this would help me to paint. I spent weeks trying to learn the properties of different colours, reading information on tubes of paint, populating spreadsheets with details and making colour charts. This stopped me from just enjoying painting and learning as I went along. A lot of time was wasted, as I couldn't remember half of the information, becoming quite confused, until I called a halt.

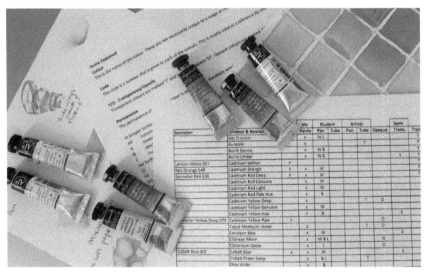

Before leaving free online resources, it's so easy to find art groups that you can join online via Face Book. If you are not a great one for participating on social media, you can just sit back and look at the vast diversity of art without having to leave home. Be inspired by the pieces you like, whilst recognising that you don't like everything.

No need to attend meetings, pay joining fees or feel out of your depth. Instagram is also a really good way of looking at other people's art, that's how I came to follow Jess and ended up taking her Loose Floral class. Instagram is at no cost, at a time convenient to you. Once you start to paint or draw, you may even enjoy putting your own work out there.

On a far grander scale, a lot of Art Galleries across the world have virtual tours. By typing into Google "Virtual Tours of Art Galleries" you can access ten of the world's best virtual museum and art gallery tours. It was only when I started art, that I found it was possible to visit the Vatican Museum in Rome, the J Paul Getty Museum in Los Angeles or the British Museum, from the comfort of my own home.

Once you have tried some of the free resources, you should have an idea of what style of art you wish to try. It's possible to purchase some very good courses; I have used Udemy, Domestika and Centre of Excellence. All three have promotions where you can get online courses from around £25. These can be viewed in your own time, paused, and watched again with access usually forever. Another online resource is Shopkeeparty, who have some free forty-five minute tutorials, mainly in watercolour and acrylic. There is also an option to purchase longer tutorials with lifetime access, or to become a patron which allows access to a larger number of tutorials. A lot of their tutorials are shown live from around the world, with recordings also made available. This does make for a more personal feeling.

If you decide to look at the Royal Academy of Arts, they have a very extensive range of courses, at various prices, including some free sketching online classes.

These are slightly different as some can be undertaken at home as live stream events. Due to the variety of courses and classes it's a good idea to check out their website to see what is currently on offer.

Getting back to actually starting art yourself, if you don't have access to online resource, there are other options. Local libraries, community newspapers or art galleries should be able to point you in the right direction for Art Groups and lessons. Local councils often run evening classes in schools, also popular are daytime classes at community hubs and events being run by local craft groups.

For those of you who may not wish to sign up for a course, there are also lots of beginner's art books. These provide very good step by step diagrams and often have outlines you can trace, if you are not ready to start drawing straight away. That way you have a template and you can practice painting the same picture with different colours, or experimenting with different techniques. There are also magazines available such as The Leisure Painter. These are much cheaper if you purchase a subscription, sometimes there are also offers to just purchase a set number of issues at a discounted price. A good idea maybe to purchase one copy, just to get an idea of the content. As well as step by step guides, you will also find interesting articles, readers' questions etc. Whilst advertisements are not usually a first reading choice, if you are new to art, they do give a good insight to the main Art Suppliers and also a range of available courses. Quite a few companies run weekend breaks with professional artists. It was from an art magazine, that I found the Watercolour Weekend with Liz, in Mapledurham, that my daughter and I both really enjoyed.

Prices for these types of events vary quite a lot, depending on the size of the class, if accommodation is needed and if materials are to be supplied. Although a class with 8 people can cost upwards from £80 for a day, the value is from having personal access to a professional artist. Attendees are usually very keen to learn as much as possible, so with a mutual passion for art, the day is both a productive and really enjoyable experience.

Having provided an insight to a variety of learning opportunities, there should be something to suit everyone. By sharing these options, you will be aware of what is out there, but it is entirely your choice whether you decide to pursue any of them. My Canal Art was almost all achieved by trial and error, learning as I went along. If you don't like sitting in front of a computer screen and are unable to attend a class, you can still be creative. If you have reached this far, something has kept you interested in the idea of starting your art. Why not pick up a pencil and draw a tea cup, then pop back to chapter 2, taking a look at my first attempt. Chances are that your first sketch is pretty similar to mine. Look again at your drawing and find the best part and the worst part. Next time you draw it, keep the good part, you can do it again, as you have already done it before. Now look at the worst part and see what you could do better next time to start improving your skills. Little steps can be all it takes, to start a great journey.

My first drawing of an eye gave the appearance of a rabbit caught in headlights, far too open and round, with too much of the eyeball showing. By looking closer, with the guidance of a free online tutorial, it was possible to make a considerable improvement.

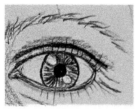 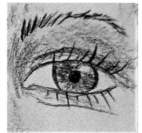 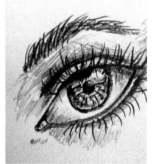

I would really recommend taking photos of your early art work, it's a great way to see how much you have moved forward, learning by doing. Comparing your own early and later work, it provides a lot of visual encouragement. Imagine what your next drawing could look like, as you continue to make progress.

With all the different types of resources available, all you need is to decide what type of art you would like to try.

Chapter 7
Exhibition Excitement

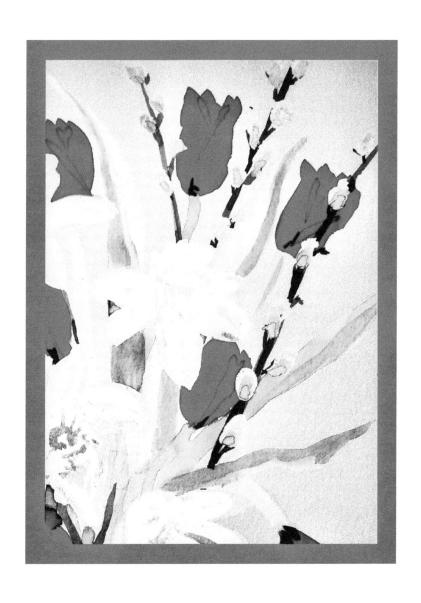

On a beautiful sunny August day, I drove to my old home town Penarth, to take flowers to the cemetery, in memory of my mum's birthday. I had grown up in this quaint old Victorian seaside town, so was unable to resist a slight detour, taking in the seafront promenade.

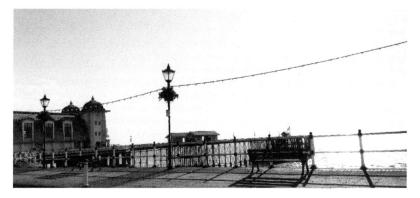

The pier had recently been refurbished, still retaining its traditional character with tall windows, roof turrets and grand entrance. with semi-circular steps and ornate pillars. The tide was in and there was a regatta underway, with all sorts of colourful yachts, tacking their way around a large course, set out in the channel.

It was Holiday Festival week, bringing back childhood memories of carnival parades and treasure hunts on the beach. Council workers would cordon off a section of the beach, pushing away the surface pebbles to reveal gritty sand. Local children would then spend hours digging for tokens, to be exchanged for lucky bags. There was always the possibility of finding an extra-large token that may even secure a family trip on the Channel Ferry.

One memory that would never fade, was participating in a maypole dance in the Italian Gardens, with the local dancing school.

There had been many hours of practice, weaving the rainbow-coloured ribbons down the pole, then skipping around and reversing the process. On the big carnival day, excitement ran high but unfortunately one of our little troop wove her long yellow ribbon the wrong way. Instead of an intricate lattice of bright satin ribbons, the maypole had become strangled, with a total tangle of colour and confusion. Music was swiftly halted and much to everyone's embarrassment, the tangle was painfully unravelled. Causing the crowding spectators to vastly swell in number, drawn by curiosity, realising something had gone wrong. Eventually the lengths of ribbon hung freely from the top of the maypole. With all eyes upon us, the music started up again and for what seemed an age, we went through the whole process again, but this time without any tangles. The audience loved it, but as young children we just wanted the ground to swallow us up. With hindsight, this was my first memorable experience of when things go wrong, have the courage to try again. Which is true of so many things, including painting.

Driving up from the promenade towards the cliff top, the Holiday Festival Art Display came into sight. Luckily a car was just pulling out of a space, recognising this as a very fortunate opportunity, I indicated and parked up. There had always been an outdoor Art Display, but as a child, balanced against the treasure hunt, donkey derby and model train ride, it hadn't really captured my attention. Time often changes how we view things. The opportunity to look at an Art Display at this point in time, was enough to make me pull over and interrupt my journey. How had I missed out on this for so long? After the treasure hunt years, there had been the teenage years, of trying to look cool and grown up, sitting in the ice-cream parlour, with a Knickerbocker glory.

Followed by dating, marriage and moving away. Only in retirement did time become available, to retrace steps and find things that had somehow been overlooked.

The Art Display was now all important. An opportunity to see so many different compositions, appreciate different styles, textures, colours and individual skills. The town council had erected a long line of zig-zag screens, for the artists to mount their art. Each had their own display area, showing their best work. Being at the seafront, there were lots of paintings depicting coastal scenes. There were beautiful tranquil skies, calm seas glistening from the suns gaze and seagulls gently floating on thermals. Others raged with stormy skies, tempestuous seas and crashing waves. All mediums were represented, oil, acrylic, watercolour, pastels, ink and pencil. Entranced by wild flowers, exotic animals and pet portraits, it was difficult to take everything in. How many years had this treasure of creativity passed me by?

Nearing the end of the exhibition, I didn't want the experience to just finish. I wanted to become part of it, to improve my art and one day proudly exhibit my flowers and animals. Nervous of showing my lack of knowledge, I had only murmured words of appreciation and pleasantries with the artists. Reaching the final display, my inner voice was shouting, these are nice people, just ask them how they became part of this, don't let the opportunity pass you by. To my relief, the last artist was about my age and gave me a warming smile, as I admired her paintings. Deep breath, the words were found at last, to ask how she had become involved with all these fabulous artists, displaying her work. The response was so much more than I could ever have expected.

Of all the artists I could have spoken to, Jilly was actually the organiser of "The Cliff Top Painters". Her enthusiasm for art was contagious and soon we were having a great conversation about the Holiday Festival Art Display.

My story tumbled out, from growing up in Penarth to starting Art in retirement. As well as being a professional artist, Jilly was the Chair of the Women's Arts Association for Wales. I had to confess I had never heard of it, but hadn't previously considered myself good enough to join any sort of Art Group, so hadn't really looked.

This group sounded perfect for me, it encouraged women artists and gave them the opportunity to exhibit their work in a non-judgemental way. Fate had caused the sun to shine that day, driving along the promenade, there had been a parking space and I had eventually met Jilly. This very ordinary August afternoon was the day that marked the next step of my art journey.

After my slight detour via the beach and long conversation with Jilly, I finally arrived at the cemetery. Although mum had passed into another dimension fourteen years ago, I still held on to her laughter and zest for life. Mum would have been so excited to think that her daughter might become one of the Cliff Top Art Display painters. All my life she had encouraged me to try things. If you don't give something a try, a great opportunity may be lost. This is so true, about starting art.

At home, settling down with a coffee, a quick Google Search brought up the Women's Arts Association for Wales. It was a very active group, referencing all sorts of exhibitions, with lots of members sharing activities that they were involved with.

Non-judgemental, as a registered charity, it offered Free Membership as well as a Full subscription for a minimal amount. There was an AGM in the autumn, with the date noted, I forwarded my enrolment and subscription. This gave access to their e-bulletin with all sorts of news and events. Meeting Jilly had given me confidence in my art and introduced me to a lot of new opportunities. With hindsight, I should have just Googled local art groups and exhibitions a long time ago. Art isn't just about exclusive viewings, multimillion pound collections and high-end investment. It's about ordinary people enjoying painting, sharing their love of art with fellow enthusiasts, joining art classes, maybe having their work on display at local charity events or possibly entering competitions. The choice of what to paint, how to paint and whether to take further steps, is entirely down to you.

As with any first event, the memory of my first piece of "exhibited art" will remain very special. With Jilly's encouragement, I put forward a painting of vibrant spring flowers, to be hung in a small local gallery. The exhibition comprised of all types of work from WAAW members. As the group had hired the gallery, there was no competition or selection process. Having no experience of art exhibitions, I was kindly advised on how to present my painting. Being a watercolour, it needed to be in a frame, edges fully secured with framing tape at the back, with flat plates on each side to enable it to be mounted on the wall. There was an allotted time for delivering pictures and receipts were given to be redeemed on collection day. Whilst at the Gallery all art was insured, to the value on the receipt. Once all the art work was handed in, volunteers organised by the committee, arranged the pieces, so they were in harmony and complemented those hung nearby.

This was quite a lengthy process, to ensure all of the art was well presented. A swell of pride mixed with disbelief brought a feeling of excitement, as my first exhibition painting was hung for all to see.

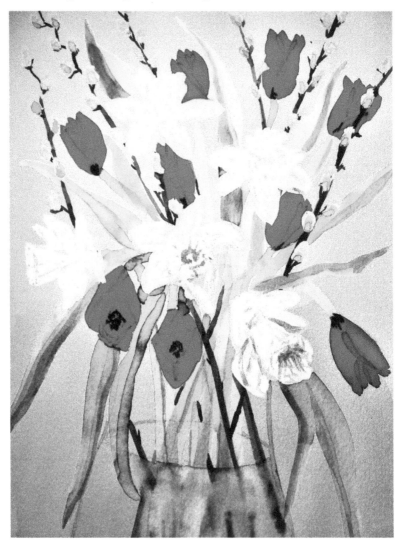

There were paintings in a variety of different mediums, in all sizes and ranging from flowers to buildings, random abstract shapes to almost anything that could be imagined. An official opening event was held, with local artists invited and light refreshments provided. It felt surreal to have people viewing my art, in a gallery, acknowledging to myself, I was now considered to be an emerging Artist. In reality, anyone who paints anything is an emerging Artist. It really doesn't matter if the art sells for a fortune or it has been painted purely for the enjoyment of being creative. Your Art is for you to enjoy, where it takes you is entirely your choice. Seeing the diversity of subject and mediums, there was no rational way to compare any of them. This reinforced the ethos of this group being non-judgemental, recognising each artistic piece as unique. Appreciation based on personal preference, would be made by those drawn to the Gallery.

Not long after I collected my spring flowers, there was a request in the e-bulletin for artwork to be donated to a local Hospice. They had been holding art auctions for several years and it had been an excellent way of fundraising. The Hospice was quite close by, so after contacting them, my painting was delivered to their fundraising team. As it had been in an exhibition, I was hoping it would be good enough to raise some money, for such a worthy cause. An activity that I had previously no knowledge of, felt like gifting something from the heart. Charity shop donations of clothing and redundant items, felt more like a recycling activity. To be able to raise money with my art was such a lovely idea.

Once again, things turned out to be on a grander scale than anticipated. There were sixty-six paintings donated, to be auctioned online.

A well known Auction House were giving their time and expertise at no cost, to support the Hospice. Prior to the Auction, invitations were sent out and the public could also register, to view and submit advanced bids. Being a totally new experience, I sat with Bob in front of our laptop, willing someone to bid on my "Spring Flowers". Bidding started at £30 and with skilful auctioneering, the hammer went down at £80. Having worried that my art wouldn't be good enough to attract a buyer, I was quite elated. Over £12,000 was raised, the top paintings being sold for a considerable amount, donated by very well-known artists. To my surprise, some paintings didn't sell and several others sold for less than mine. The event really helped to raise my confidence. This is now on my "to do" list, for as many years as the fundraising Art Auction continues. A double benefit, enjoying painting and a worthy cause benefiting from its sale.

Two other exhibitions were also being arranged by the WAAW. Deciding to put forward a peacock, inspired by several photographs I had taken, I was no longer apprehensive. As your painting eye for detail improves, your eye for taking photos also improves. Using a smart phone, it's possible to take a vast quantity of pictures, to enable a good composition to be captured. An excellent tip, once a particular shot has been chosen; reproduce it in black and white, making it a lot easier to identify the light and dark tones. This was really helpful when painting my peacock. The colours can be referenced from the original photo, or can be adjusted to suit your creative mood. Another useful tip is to paint the eyes first. Certainly, one of the hardest and most important parts to painting, when trying to give animals and birds character.

If you get the eyes right, the rest will follow. Imagine spending ages on peacock feathers, beak and head, only to have a problem with the eyes.

It's so easy to do a few practice eyes, and then decide on what looks best for your painting. Again, the internet is great for looking at different types of eyes. Some have large dark circular pupils whilst others have narrow, vertical, oval pupils. Get the right eyes and you are well on your way to a great bird or animal.

Handing in my peacock was an exciting moment. A real sense of achievement, that my art was to be part of a diverse exhibition of paintings, to be hung in a large public gallery adjoining a library. Consider how you might feel if it was your painting. Excited, pleased, humbled, elated, a passion for painting can create a lot of emotion, which is so rewarding. Having been exhibited, my peacock is heading off to a new home via the Annual Hospice Auction.

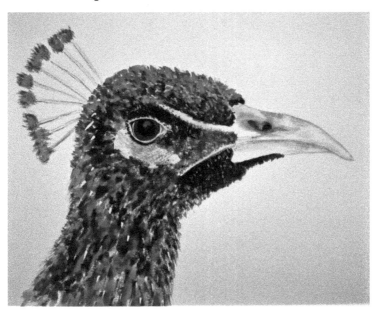

Another surprise, arrangements were put in place for a video to be made of the exhibition, which could be accessed online. It was quite surreal to click the link in the WAAW e-bulletin, then see my peacock appear in a virtual tour. I had viewed virtual tours of art galleries and museums, but never imagined I would have my art online. Nothing can compare with being so close to art, that you can see brushstrokes on canvas, appreciate the delicate transparency of watercolours, feel the texture of acrylics, all whilst your eyes are drawn around the various exhibits. However, virtual tours do give access to art work all over the world, which is a fantastic place of reference. If you are just starting to paint, many sites have links to other sites; suddenly a whole new world of virtual art is just waiting to be viewed

My third exhibition piece was my winning Pink Orchid. A little unsure of what to submit, I stayed safe. Flowers and birds being my favourite things to paint, they were at the heart of my passion. As well as paintings, there were also various crafts and sculptures at this exhibition. By looking at lots of different styles of art, you can begin to develop your own personal style. After years in Finance, having to pay great attention to detail, I really enjoyed art that showed the detail found in nature, particularly flowers, trees, birds and animals. I soon realised that random patterns and expressive shapes didn't come naturally. To get the most out of your art, it's important to paint things that ignite a passion. Whilst it is possible to appreciate the skills of others, there is no point in tasking yourself to learn how to paint a portrait, if you would feel much more excited about painting a horse. If a subject interests you, automatically you feel more comfortable, relaxed, keen to observe the detail and capture its essence on paper or canvas.

When you start painting, find something that really interests you. Life would be pretty dull if everyone painted the same things, in the same way. Art is all about being creative. Experiment, you may be one of the super creative people, who can express feelings of anger and joy with random marks and clashing colours. Personally, I would really struggle with that level of disorder, as my personality revolves around accuracy, creating order and remaining calm. Someone who likes surprises, new experiences and being spontaneous, would see the world with different eyes and therefore may enjoy painting with less detail and order. It's all down to choice, indulge your creativity and let loose the artist in you.

Confidence gradually increasing, I became a Committee Member of the WAAW. This was a great way to learn about the nuts and bolts of the art world, as well as giving some time in return, for all the valuable things I was learning. Considering something like this, you may wonder what you could contribute, if you have very little background in Art. Rest assured, someone is always needed to take minutes, collate articles submitted for newsletters & media posts, as well as helping with event activities.

If you have the time, being involved with an art group is very rewarding. Others are really keen to share their knowledge and you will be surprised how your own life skills can be beneficial to other members. Every artist started to paint at some time, this is your time, let my passion for painting encourage you. It's never too late to start your art.

Chapter 8
Talking Art

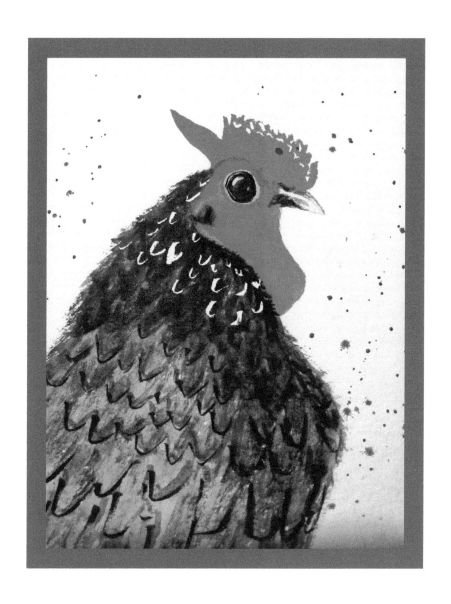

There are two elements to this chapter, both of which fall nicely under the title of Talking Art. Starting my art led to meeting a lot of very interesting people. Karin is a professional artist, who seems to have a vast number of connections. Always busy painting, selling her work, whilst still finding time to be involved with local community projects and events. Karin has a passion for anything Welsh, as well as chickens, which prompted my choice of title art work.

Karin runs an Art Group, and thought members would be interested to hear about my art journey. How our narrow boat restoration resulted in me painting canal roses, which then led to watercolour art, sketching and many interesting activities. Before retirement, my role had involved presentations to some quite large audiences, so I was reasonably comfortable with the idea. My only concern was the content of my talk. As someone with no formal art qualifications, relatively new to painting, could I hold the interest of an audience for fifty minutes?

I forwarded an outline to Karin, along with pictures of our boat taken during the refurbishment. I was keen to use the opportunity to encourage people to try different styles of art, by comparing my very wobbly first attempts with my later improved artwork. There was also the worry of seeming too basic with illustrations or making it appear that I was just using it as an opportunity to show off my art. As Karin appeared happy with my outline, a firm date for the talk was agreed. No going back now or I would be letting people down

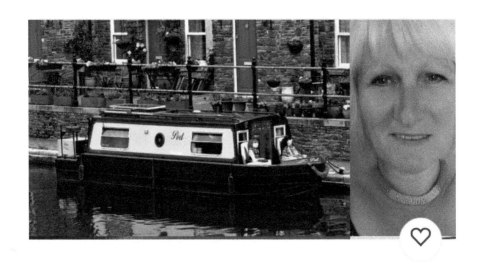

Karin's Arts Club with Sue Trusler, Artist

To put together the talk, I tried to look at it from the point of view of my audience. Without knowing me, some may wish to have a little background information, but wouldn't want a full plotted life history. Those with no experience of narrowboats would need an introduction to being on a canal, but not every detail of mooring techniques and rope tying. As most of my audience would have some painting or drawing skills, they would be keen to hear of the process used for painting canal roses. As a somewhat forgotten skill, it would be unlikely that anyone had tried it. That gave an opportunity to start with the very basic process of painting canal art roses, then expanding into the design detail. Timing played a big part in getting things right. Too much content and something may be rushed at the end or the whole talk may overwhelm, with information overload. Too little content and the talk could lose pace and peter out at the end.

With tickets sold and content sorted all that was needed was a run through the technical bits, as this was to be live via zoom. With backups of pictures, technical glitches sorted and timing rehearsed, all was ready for the event.

On the day, the technical bits all worked well, alleviating my biggest fear. There is nothing worse than connection issues, people unable to hear the host, or having difficulty logging in. With a small clock next to my laptop, spot on the hour I started to talk. What I failed to anticipate in all my preparation was that I couldn't see any of my audience. I was talking to my laptop about pictures on my screen. Looking back at me was a small square mirror image of myself talking in the top right corner of the screen. Whether presenting to small groups or large audiences, I had always been able to judge how my words were being received. I could adjust my pace or add a little humour.

Now I had nothing. Was there actually anyone out there at all? Just because there were a number of participants showing in the display bar, on the bottom of the screen, they may have all gone off to make a coffee or feed the cat. I suddenly felt very alone. No time to pause, this was live. I needed to imagine a virtual audience, erasing the surrounding walls and furniture of my dining room. It may have had the best Wi-Fi connection in our home, but it certainly didn't mimic a setting full of people, listening intently, to an interesting talk. Mentally focusing on my virtual audience, I progressed through my story, eventually arriving at the final sentence, " it's never too late to start your art". I'd made it to the end, spot on time. Closing my screen share, a sigh of relief, the real audience appeared in square images, with smiles on their faces.

There was time for a short Q&A session, whilst lots of very positive and encouraging comments went into the chat. I was quite taken aback by the interest, with the overriding factor being identified as my enthusiasm and willingness to share my experiences honestly.

As with everything to do with art, this opened up yet another chapter. If I could engage with people by talking to a screen in my dining room, then I should be able to engage with far more people by writing a book. A seed was sown; hopefully you are now enjoying reading this book. My passion for art continues to grow, a passion that is also easy for you to embrace and enjoy.

Having gained your interest, its time to talk a little about the equipment needed to make that start.

The second element of this chapter is all about materials and techniques. There is a vast amount of information available, as discussed in Chapter 6, What's Out There. If you intend painting or drawing for pleasure, I hope it will be helpful to share some of the things that I have learnt. At the end of the chapter, you will find lists of the materials required for the relevant art style of each chapter.

PAPER

A whole book could easily be written on different types of paper and their properties. Here you will find the basic details which are sufficient for you to start painting. The very best watercolour paper is made by hand from 100% cotton fibre and is acid free. Most papers are made from wood pulp or a mix of wood pulp with cotton fibres.

Paper comes in a vast range of sizes, if you are thinking of framing some of your work, it's a good idea to look at frame sizes and match your paper accordingly. It can become quite frustrating if you paint something and it is either a bit too tall or too narrow to fit a popular size frame.

Paper is sold by individual sheets, by the roll, in pads, joined at one edge ranging from 10 to 50 sheets or in blocks. My preference is blocks, as the sheets are sealed together on all 4 edges, with a small gap left to insert a blade, to separate the paper once a painting is complete. This helps to keep the paper flat and avoid buckling.

Watercolour paper comes in different weights, the most common being 185gsm, 300gsm and 640gsm. My preference is normally 300gsm.

The lightest or thinnest is not suitable for use with too much water or too many layers of paint. If used, it is often stretched prior to painting, to reduce the chance of buckling. There are several different processes, the main aim being to wet the paper, attach it to a stiff board with masking tape and allow it to dry. There are many different approaches to doing this. Painting for pleasure, I found stretching paper a bit messy and time consuming, so just buy heavier paper to start with. Heavier paper will also tolerate more applications or glazes of paint. Where paint is applied, left to dry and further applications made to create depth of colour.

The surface texture of paper will determine how the paint flows and settles.

Hot Pressed (HP) is the smoothest paper, often used for botanical art and detailed work. Paint will flow smoothly and fine detail can be easily painted.

Cold Pressed (NOT) is slightly textured for general all round use.

Rough is highly textured and best suited to expressive work.

As with many things, it is very much down to personal preference. If you are on a limited budget, it is better to buy good quality paper and slightly less expensive paints and brushes. The geese below were all painted on the same afternoon with the same paints and brushes, using different quality paper.

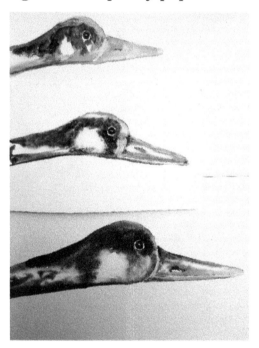

It may seem an absolute bargain to purchase a book with fifty sheets of "watercolour paper" for the same price as twenty sheets of a recognised quality brand. Before you do, think of my geese. The top is the cheapest paper, where the paint didn't flow and blend.

On the best paper at the bottom, the paint has reacted well and produced a soft blend of tones. Until I tried it, I had no idea what a difference using a good paper could make. I like Archers, Bockingford and Daler Rowney. Some large art suppliers such as Cass Art and Jackson's Art market a range of their own papers which are reasonably priced and perform well. It's worth waiting for sales which are often a great time to stock up on supplies.

BRUSHES

Brushes come in all shapes and sizes, with round ends, pointed ends, long handles, short handles, made from a range of synthetic and animal hair. Prices for one brush can range from £1.50 to over £100. To start painting with watercolour, your first decision is whether your art is going to be small and detailed or large and loose. This will give some indication of the size and shape of brushes you require.

PAINTS, INKS & PENCILS

There are so many types, brands & colours of paint, inks and pencils, it could easily leave you in a state of confusion. To keep things straight forward, the basic requirements are shown below for the style of art in each chapter.

CHAPTER 1 CANAL ART - ACRYLICS

Acrylic paints are best used for this style of art. They are most commonly sold in metal or plastic tubes. It's important to clean residue from around the tube before tightening the top back on. This stops the top sticking, possibly causing the cap to break when you try to open it a few days later.

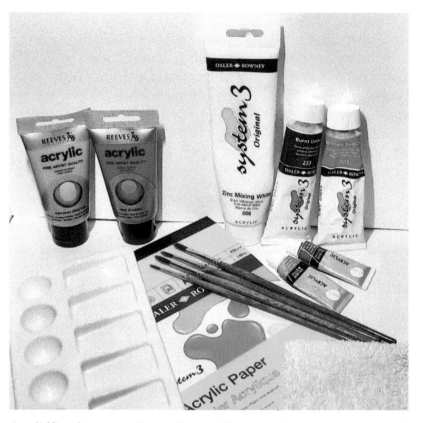

It is difficult to seal a tube well enough to stop the paint drying, if you break the cap.

Acrylic paint dries quite swiftly when exposed to the air, so it is best only to squeeze onto a pallet an estimated amount required for a specific piece of work.

If you are painting tin cans, ensure they are fully clean otherwise the paint won't adhere to the surface. If you prefer to paint on paper, it's best to purchase paper that is specifically for acrylic paint. I have found that acrylic paint can be used with most clean surfaces. I have painted wooden spoons and metal flowerpots. Once fully dry, it's a good idea to coat with a clear varnish.

126

Brushes should be for acrylic paint, although some are suitable for both acrylic and watercolour. Brush size depends on how large you intend your artwork to be. For my canal art roses I used size 2, 4, 6 and a ¼ flat brush.

There are two very important pieces of guidance when using acrylic paint. Firstly, rinse your brush in water regularly, otherwise the paint starts to dry on the brush and won't adhere to your painting surface. Second, is never to leave your brush standing in a jar of water. This bends the bristles and distorts the shape of the brush. It's a good idea to have some kitchen roll to hand, as well as a spare piece of paper to try out colours. Acrylic paints can be mixed together. If you are looking to lighten a colour, then the properties of Zinc Mixing White, make it very good for this purpose. There is a Titanium White, which is better suited to painting on top of other colours once they are dry.

Acrylic paint can be mixed with a little water straight from the tube. Once exposed to the air it does start to dry quite rapidly on a sunny day. Your pallet should be cleaned whilst the paint is still wet. If not, leave it dry fully and you can peel off the paint.

CHAPTER 2 BOTANICAL BEAUTY - WATERCOLOURS

Botanical art taught by Debbie, uses watercolours that can be purchased in tubes or pans. My little pan set was great to start off with. You don't need a vast array of colours and the paints last quite well. A small amount of water will reactivate them.

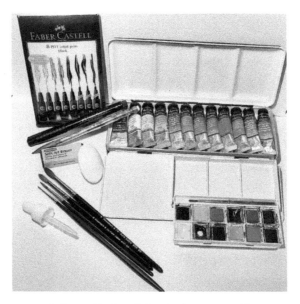

As I progressed, I switched to tubes, as they can be mixed more easily in a pallet and last a long time. Student quality are cheaper than Artist or Professional paint as there is less pigment in the manufacturing process. I would prefer to have six Artist paints than twelve Student paints. The initial temptation is to buy lots of different colours, however you can make a range of your own, by mixing the primary colours, red, blue & yellow. Unlike acrylics, the way to make watercolour paint lighter is not to add white, but to add water. The more water the more diluted and lighter the colour becomes. A deep scarlet with lots of water added can become a light pink.

Due to the delicate nature of Botanical Art, in the main, the brushes used are quite small and are specifically made for watercolour. A good range to start with would be No. 00 as well as no. 5,6 & 8. Again, a clean brush is important to avoid muddy colours, so you will need two water pots, one to swish a paint laden brush in to clean, the other for dampening paper and using to dilute your paint.

The preferred paper is HP (Hot Pressed) as this is very smooth and ideal for painting detail. The outline of your subject can be drawn with any pencil that is not too hard. No one wants indentations on the paper after the pencil line has been erased. When the time comes to carefully erase lines, I use a cheap fluffy brush, to sweep off the eraser residue, rather than brushing with my hands which may be a little oily and leave fingerprints. It's worth getting a good eraser, some cheaper ones are made of plastic and can easily disturb the structure of your paper. A great way to start painting Botanical Art is to draw a pencil outline and when you are comfortable with it, go over the drawing with a fine permanent ink pen. Always ensure it is fully dry before painting near to the ink lines.

Kitchen roll is always handy to have around, I also use a small eye dropper to add water to a pallet, it is an easy way to control the amount of water you are adding to dilute a colour.

My biggest tip is that you can keep paint in a pallet for using another day. It dries out but can be livened up with just a little water. Freezer bags can be used to store individual pallets, which can then be revived as required. From trying to analyse every possible property of each specific colour, I now love just blending them together, adding water and introducing other shades until I arrive at what I want. This is where an old piece of paper is really handy

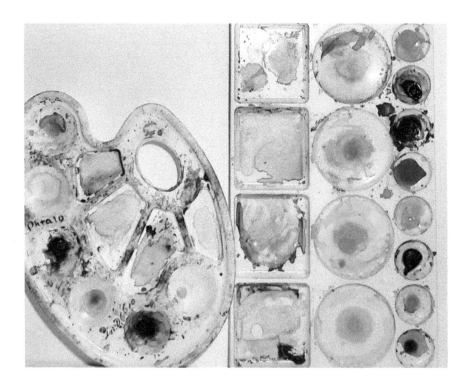

These two pallets have had small amounts of paint from tubes placed into some of the wells. The larger areas have then been used to mix different colours and dilute them if a lighter shade is needed. They look rather messy but are quite practical and saves wasting paint.

If you would prefer not to use plastic, china pallets are available or you can use a large white china dinner plate. Dotting the paint around the edge. Over a period of time, plastic pallets do stain, whereas china remains white.

CHAPTER 3 SKETCHING SKILLS - PENCILS

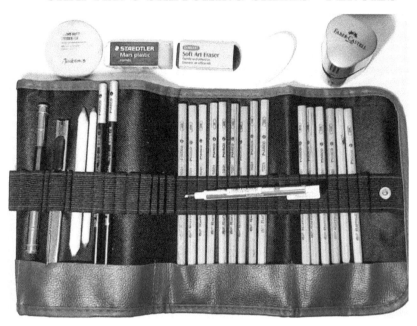

As a minimum, it's possible to begin sketching with three pencils, HB, 2B and 4B. With a sketch book, sharpener and eraser you have all that is needed to start being creative.

I must confess, after the first week of my sketching course, I did invest in a roll of assorted pencils and then just had to try them all out. There is a huge difference between hard and soft pencils. My roll also contained some smudging sticks, made of white paper they are used to blend pencil marks. Cotton buds could be used as a substitute.

Also included was a metal tube, to hold your pencil in when it is short and nearly run out. Next was a small knife, which could have several uses, including sharpening pencils, or releasing art paper blocks. The final items were charcoal pencils, beware, they can smudge everywhere.

If you ever decide to use them, a good tip is to rest your drawing hand on a tissue, to avoid smudging your work. Needless to say, a few erasers are really useful, my greatest find was a small eraser that operated like a propelling pencil. The beauty of this was that very small areas could be easily targeted.

CHAPTER 4 WATERCOLOUR WEEKEND

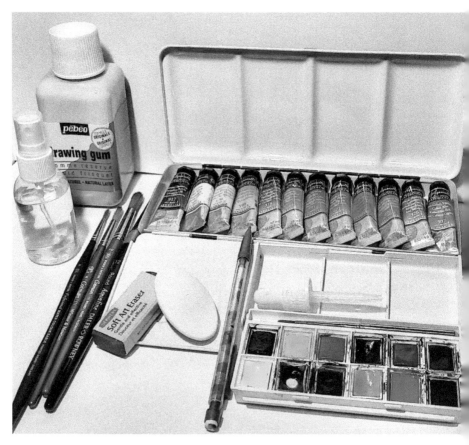

Materials here are similar to the Botanical art, except the basic brushes are larger. This time we are looking at sizes 3, 6,10 & 12. Again, brushes need to be cleaned regularly so two pots of water are called for.

White masking fluid is required or my favourite, blue Pebeo Drawing Gum. Remember an old or cheap brush for application. Both serve the same purpose and can be carefully rolled off the paper when the appropriate time has arrived, as in the cherry tree painting, after the background had been completed and dried. There is also an eraser for this task called a Maskaway eraser, which is quite solid and has an uneven pitted surface. I purchased one but found it easier to use my fingers to roll the gum off. The final addition to this style of watercolour is a small water spritzer bottle. It can be used for several processes, to dampen paper, spray over painted areas or used to lightly spray paint pans, to revive them. Paper for this type of art is usually NOT (Not Hot Pressed) or rough, however the choice is yours.

CHAPTER 5 LOOSE FLORALS - INKS

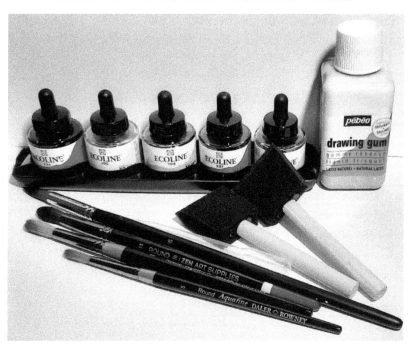

Here we switch over to ink, not permanent ink pens, but bottles of watercolour inks that are transparent dye based and can be mixed together and diluted with water. As well as large watercolour brushes, size 8, 11, 12 & 16 foam brush sponges are also needed. These are foam wedges attached to pencil length sticks. They come in various sizes and are usually sold in packs of five for around £5. The ink bottles have quite narrow necks so it is best to put small amounts of ink into separate containers. Small beakers or recycled yoghurt pots are ideal.

Pebeo drawing gum or masking fluid is a key part of this style of art, preserving large white areas. When applying to large areas, try to put sweeping strokes in one direction, rather than going back and forth over the same area, as this dries quickly and you could end up pulling some of it away. To apply masking fluid, you need an old brush, never use a good brush or it will be ruined. Also make sure you keep swooshing in water to avoid the masking fluid sticking to your brush.

EXTRA INFORMATION

Having covered the basic requirements for trying the various types of art, by chapter, there are some very exciting watercolour products out there.

Watercolour pencils, look like normal pencils, except after drawing something, you can use a wet brush with clean water to go over the pencil marks. These then melt into a liquid paint. They can be blended like paint and are mostly more vibrant when dampened.

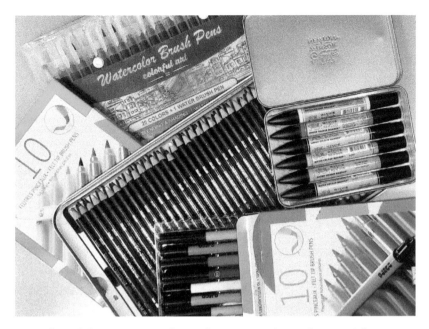

To make this even easier, there are brushes with barrels that can be filled with water, so no need to even have a jar of water. Great if you want to be creative on a day out. With a small watercolour pad, watercolour pencils and a loaded brush, you are all set up.

In my childhood it was a great novelty to have a packet of felt pens. Times have moved on and it is now possible to have coloured brush pens. These can be used like a paintbrush by just removing the lid and painting. They can be dipped in water to make a lighter shade and blended together.

Having used black permanent pens of different thicknesses for botanical art, I then discovered coloured permanent pens. There are also an endless variety of coloured marker pens, with pointed, rounded and wedge shaped ends.

Curbing my desire to try everything out there, I haven't as yet sampled the endless range of pastel pencils & crayons, metallic pencils, two tone-coloured pencils, along with a host of interesting products that keep being developed.

I was tempted by some of the mediums that can be added to watercolour paint. These products can slow down the drying time, giving longer time to work. They can also create a granular effect, adding texture to your painting. My favourite is the Iridescent medium which can be mixed with watercolour to create a pearly sheen.

Once you have entered the world of Art, an Aladdin's cave of all things creative becomes available. I cannot resist trying out new colours, different style brushes, as well as trying exciting new techniques.

It is my greatest wish that having read this book, you will now be keen to start your own art journey. Good Luck and enjoy your creativity.

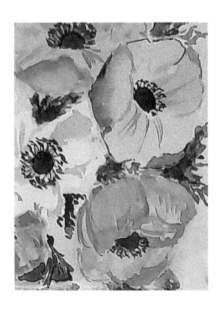

Acknowledgements

Thank you to all who have imparted their knowledge and inspired me to write this book. Thanks also to Choir Press for their publishing guidance.

A special thanks to my husband Bob and daughter Rachel, for being part of my journey, providing encouragement and support.

Professional Artists

Debbie Devauden - Botanical Art
http://debbiedevauden.co.uk/
Rhiannon Powell - Sketching Skills
Instagram rhiannonpowell27
Liz Chaderton - Watercolour Weekend,
https://lizchaderton.co.uk
Jess Priest – Loose Florals,
www.texintel.com/designdirectory/jess-priest
Jilly Hicks – Exhibition Excitement
Karin Mear – Talking Art
https://karinmear.com/
Shiree Stainer,
www.facebook.com/ShireeStainerDesignerCreative
EducatorMentor

Mentors

Women's Arts Association Wales.
https://womensarts.co.uk/
Michael Heppells Write That Book Masterclass
Rob Townsend, website design
https://robtownsend.com/
My cousin Julie and many friends who have helped proof read chapters.

Lightning Source UK Ltd.
Milton Keynes UK
UKHW020845221021
392603UK00002B/5